RUNNING THE CORPORATE OFFENSE

Lessons in Effective Leadership *from the* Bench *to the* Board Room

Mat Ishbia

ENVISION BOOKS

Library of Congress Cataloguing-in-Publication Data available upon request

This book is available in quantity at special discounts for your group or organization. For further information, contact:

Envision Books
An imprint of Triumph Books LLC
814 North Franklin Street
Chicago, Illinois 60610
(312) 337-0747
www.triumphbooks.com

Printed in U.S.A.
ISBN: 978-1-62937-990-6
Design by Patricia Frey

CONTENTS

FOREWORD

WHEN YOU COACH COLLEGE BASKETBALL AND LEAD groups of young men for as long as I have, you become good at sensing who people are *beyond* the game. You can see past things like how high someone can jump or how good of a shooter they are from behind the arc, and really see someone's potential as a leader and as a person. It becomes easy to spot people who have "it."

Some guys are destined for great careers playing professional basketball. Others might not be at that level athletically, but they can be game-changers in a variety of other ways, whether it's coaching, teaching, running a company, starting a foundation, whatever it is.

The NCAA talks about the "thousands of student-athletes that go pro in something other than sports," and seeing that come to fruition is one of the most fulfilling parts of my job every year. It's so rewarding to see my guys chase their passions and career dreams the same way we have them chase conference championships and national championships at Michigan State.

Mat Ishbia is one of those special guys that I'm proud to have as part of our Michigan State basketball family.

He has been a truly great alum of Michigan State University. Mat joined our basketball program as a walk-on, and he graduated as a five-star person and business professional.

Mat wasn't born to be some sort of dominant athletic specimen. It wasn't in his DNA to be 6-foot-5 or have a 40-inch vertical jump, but he was born and raised to be a workhorse. He's a great example of the level of effort I want my players to give on a daily basis, just like he's an example of how successful collegiate student-athletes can be outside of basketball.

Mat became a leader at United Wholesale Mortgage when it was small, like your typical "mom and pop" shop, and grew it into one of the biggest mortgage companies in the country. If you know Mat, that growth and success isn't even a bit surprising. I saw firsthand how driven and competitive he was for five years, both as a player and a coach. He didn't fill the stat sheet on game night, but he consistently raised the level of our entire team's play, day in and day out.

Mat might have joined our Michigan State program as a walk-on, but I could tell early on that he had all the mental tools needed to be a successful leader, regardless of what path he ultimately chose. It was easy to look into his eyes and see that he had that drive that fuels the fiercest of competitors. He was the kind of guy that hated to lose and wanted to be the best.

Quite frankly, when I looked at Mat, I saw a little bit of myself.

He was smaller than a lot of people but had the drive and the grit to always compete. He would never back down from anyone. He'd play physical and throw his body around and make all the hustle plays. Mateen Cleaves was the best point guard in the country, and not to disrespect anyone else who played during that era, but I'm not sure anyone in the country gave Mateen fits like Mat did in practice every day.

It's an honor, for me and our program, that Mat has been so successful in life. He was a big part of our team that helped us win three Big Ten championships, a national championship, and made three Final Fours, and I knew that big things were in store for him. I'm glad that our program has played a part in his success, with Mat incorporating philosophies and habits of ours into United Wholesale Mortgage, it's even better that he's used that Spartan mindset to win multiple "national championships" as the No. 1 wholesale mortgage lender in the country.

Once upon a time, Mat Ishbia was an 18-year-old kid grinding every day and working hard to be the glue guy that stuck our team together. Now he's a legitimate superstar in the business world. I can assure you, if you're an up-and-comer with aspirations of becoming a leader and growing your own business, follow Mat's lead.

There isn't one person I've coached who is more game-ready when it comes to running the corporate offense. In Mat, I saw a player who was not the most talented but always gave it his all until the buzzer sounded. He never relaxed. You could see how badly he cared about winning every single day at practice. Mat always put the team first. He was a winner, and more than anything, made me believe that he would achieve success in whatever he touched. Winners win at anything they do. Mat Ishbia is one of the ultimate winners!

Tom Izzo
Head Men's Basketball Coach
Michigan State University

1

BASKETBALL GUIDES ME

TICK-TOCK. TICK-TOCK. THERE WE WERE, INCHING CLOSER and closer to crunch time. It was the third quarter with the national championship on the line and we were down—within striking distance, sure, but still with a pretty decent gap to close against a team that was the defending champions.

What was going to push us over the top? What strategic adjustment could we make heading into the fourth quarter that would shift all the momentum in our favor? It was going to be up to me to make it happen, and my teammates believed in me.

For years it had been a personal goal of mine to reach this point, and our team had collectively worked its tail off to get here, but things look different when you're actually in that moment.

I thought to myself, "What am I going to say to rally this group of people?"

I knew that leaders can't waver in moments of stress. No flinching or second-guessing is allowed when the big game is on the line. You've got to make a decision and run with it—and then hope you were right.

So, in the middle of the huddle, with my teammates circled around me hanging on every word, I drew up the perfect game plan for that fourth quarter. I looked every person in the eyes and told them without an ounce of doubt in my voice what we were going to do. We were going to methodically come back to win the championship. That No. 1 slot was ours, it was just a matter of time.

As the leader, I had to exude that confidence, regardless of how likely the rest of the team thought our chances were. And as we broke from the huddle, I just hoped like hell it would work.

This was it—crunch time. My adrenaline was pumping. I felt like my heart was going to beat right out of my chest. I was nervous, not only because a year's worth of hard work was coming down to the final quarter of action, but also because I had gotten my teammates to buy in to my vision of victory. If we didn't pull out the win, would they *really* believe in me ever again?

That's a big risk.

As I got back into the action with my "win at all costs" teammates, I imagined our opponents beating their chests and gearing up for a celebration that wasn't going to happen. Pride comes before the fall, and I was going to savor every moment of being the team that put them in their place.

If our opponent was overconfident, I can't really blame them. They were a juggernaut, crushing every competitor in their path. They had essentially been living at the top of the rankings and no one had even come close to challenging them. They were a lock to win the national championship again. They were like a team of grown men playing against boys.

Because they had dominated the competition all year long, which wasn't anything new or special to them, they didn't even realize there was another team playing for the championship. They underestimated the mindset and motivation of a hungry program full of players sick and tired of not winning. That's what we were.

Contending for a national championship was the very pinnacle of our dreams; it was our reason for existing. We walked, talked, ate, and slept thinking of winning the title, whereas it had become routine for our opponent. And, boy, did it show in that fourth quarter.

We sped things up and pushed the pedal to the metal the entire time. We didn't even give them time to react. It felt like they were frozen in place while we ran laps around them. We stormed right by them. Down by just a bit to start the quarter, we blew past them and ended up winning the national championship by one.

One billion, that is.

With a strong fourth quarter, our team became the No. 1 wholesale mortgage lender in the country, turning an $80 million deficit after three quarters into a victory of $1 billion. We were national champions for the first time in 2015, accomplishing the goal I had set for the Company since I became president of United Wholesale Mortgage six years earlier. We haven't budged from the No. 1 spot since.

If you thought that opening scene was about a basketball game, I wouldn't blame you. It would make complete sense, given my background. I was a point guard on the Michigan State University basketball team for four years, from 1998 to 2002, under famed head coach Tom Izzo. During that time our team won three Big Ten championships, made three NCAA Final Four appearances, and won the NCAA national championship in 2000.

You Don't Have to Be Captain to Be a Leader

I was on the team, but by no means was I a star at Michigan State. Not even close. People used to compare me to the cigar legendary Boston Celtics coach Red Auerbach would puff when he knew his team had clinched a win—saying I was like a human victory cigar. When I came onto the floor, you knew the game had already been chalked up as a win.

But that wasn't my most important role. Although I wasn't the captain of the team, I was one of the leaders. The 15th man on a basketball team isn't typically who the other players look to for leadership, but all those highly touted guys that I was teammates with—Mateen Cleaves, Jason Richardson, Morris Peterson, and others—viewed me as a leader.

Leadership doesn't require you to be the most talented player on your team or to have all the answers. You don't have to be the biggest, fastest, or strongest guy in the locker room. People demonstrate leadership in a variety of ways. There isn't one box you have to check. No right or wrong answer.

Regardless of your personal leadership style, there is one characteristic that you must demonstrate. At your core, in order to be a leader, you have to be someone that people are willing to listen to and follow. You've got to be a living example of how things should be done.

That's how I was able to be a leader on the Michigan State basketball team despite being the last guy on the bench. Not only was I someone that strived to give 100 percent effort at all times, I tried to be a good teammate. I built strong relationships with everyone on the team and was someone that people felt comfortable talking to about anything. I was respected, not only because I busted my butt every day, but because I did it all for the greater good of the team.

I cared more for the "Michigan State" on the front of my jersey than the "Ishbia" on the back. More than anything else, I wanted to be a great teammate, and worked hard to demonstrate that I was worthy of being there.

I grew up in suburban Detroit, lived in one of the best school districts, and was the star basketball player on my team at Seaholm High School in Birmingham, Michigan, averaging 23 points per game. Both of my parents worked. My mother was a teacher in Pontiac, Michigan. My father was an attorney who doubled as a serial entrepreneur. He founded several companies, the largest of which, by far, is United Wholesale Mortgage—the Company where I'm president and CEO today.

But as I was headed off to East Lansing to play for the Spartans, I knew that other guys on the team didn't have the same economic advantages that I did. I understood that guys on the team couldn't relate to where I came from, but I wanted to make sure we related to each other completely where it mattered the most—on the court and in the locker room.

I took that mindset to the extreme. Before I left for college, like many parents, my father generously bought me a used car to take to school.

But I refused to keep it because I thought it'd make me stand out from guys on the basketball team who didn't have a car.

Fitting in was way more important to me than showing off what I had. I wanted to be part of the program, not stand out. I made sure I wasn't seen as "Mat Ishbia from Birmingham," but Mat Ishbia, the ultimate team player who gave 100 percent effort every day, had great relationships with everyone, and honored the green-and-white jersey he was fortunate enough to wear.

Fast-forwarding a few years, I see that same concept of relatability and team spirit as integral to my success as a leader. Connecting with people, building strong relationships, and committing total support to the team's efforts.

I try very hard not to be like CEOs who hide away in some top-floor corner office and are rarely seen by anyone outside the executive leadership team. I don't drive a flashy car and I don't have a big wardrobe.

I'm a normal guy who does the same things as other people in their 30s. I eat lunch at Taco Bell. I play fantasy football and talk trash with my buddies every week.

Sure, I carry myself professionally and take my responsibilities as the CEO of a multi-billion-dollar Company very seriously, but more importantly, I view myself as just another one of the guys on the team. I know I'm not better than anyone just because I'm the CEO. I'm just another teammate playing his role, working hard to make the Company great.

Despite that, I didn't always plan to enter the mortgage business. Growing up, basketball was really all I cared about. I always had a ball in my hands, whether it was for the school team, a pickup game at a neighborhood park, or some one-on-one in the driveway. If I wasn't playing basketball, I was watching it.

When I graduated from Michigan State with a degree in business management, I still had a lot to learn about business. And I certainly didn't know anything about the mortgage business.

But when it came down to it, after four years of playing basketball at Michigan State and one year of serving as a student assistant coach on Coach Izzo's staff, I passed on continuing my basketball career.

I had the opportunity to join Mike Garland's staff at Cleveland State University, which would have made me, at age

23, the youngest Division I assistant coach that year, but instead chose to join the Company that my father had started when I was six years old.

Wait, what?

How did a guy who loved everything about the game of basketball and admittedly didn't know anything about mortgages make that decision?

I Could Always Go Back to Basketball

Ultimately, it came down to two conversations—one with Coach Izzo and the other with my father.

I distinctly remember Coach Izzo telling me that I could try out the business scene and if it wasn't the best fit, I could always go back to basketball. In retrospect, it seems kind of funny to think of a career in basketball as something to fall back on, but he suggested that this could be an opportunity for me to do something special by applying the principles and strategies I learned from the Michigan State basketball program to the business world.

That comment has always resonated with me. I remember thinking that I had never imagined business could be the same as basketball.

I had the second conversation with my father shortly after. He was fully supportive and didn't pressure me one way or the other. But, of course he loved the idea of me joining his Company and helping it grow.

I definitely had my doubts. I told him, "Dad, I'm too competitive. I need to have that rush, that intensity." That was obviously the basketball player in me talking.

It's hard to go from years of fast-paced excitement—winning championships and sharing the brotherhood that comes from basketball—to suddenly being an office guy that wears a suit and sits at a desk.

Try this. Lace up your shoes and run some five-on-five action for a few hours at your local rec center or YMCA, and then immediately head over to the library to play around with a Microsoft Excel spreadsheet for a couple hours. Then tell me which one is more fun.

That's how I thought of it, at least. But my father said to me, "Mat, come work in the mortgage business for a year and you'll see that you can apply that competitiveness here and do amazing things in any business. If you have that drive to be successful, you'll fall in love with the mortgage business just like you did with basketball."

He couldn't have been more right. That's exactly what happened. Strange as it may sound, I fell in love with mortgages.

You might think that mortgages sound boring. How could mortgages *possibly* compare to basketball?

You'd be surprised. What's driven me throughout my career is that the mortgage business isn't *just* about mortgages—it's about making a difference in peoples' lives and helping make their dreams come true. It's about creating jobs and giving people opportunities. Of course, there's also the thrill of snatching away a prospective client from a competitor.

To this day, basketball is in my blood and that competitive itch is alive and well. I've been able to productively channel that energy because the mortgage business is actually structured very much like basketball. It's competitive and allows you to track wins and losses against your rivals. But in this case, instead of other schools or sports teams throughout a season, you're going up against other lenders every day.

Like a good basketball team, we scout our competition. We aim to out-recruit our competitors to bring in top talent. There's a consistent focus on "player development," and giving your people the best possible tools and training so they can maximize their abilities and production. There are year-long rankings and a clear-cut No. 1 at the end of the year—akin to a "national champion."

The competition to be No. 1 in the mortgage business is fierce, and it is completely objective. There isn't any voting. No polls that a committee meets to discuss. No opportunity for a team that didn't win its conference championship to win the title. There's an actual No. 1 mortgage lender in the country every year.

You Have to Have a Game Plan

The spirit of basketball drives my behavior and leadership style every day and is apparent even in the language our Company uses.

We don't have employees at United Wholesale Mortgage, we have team members." You won't find anyone with a business card that has the word "manager" on it. Instead, we have team captains around the building and many teams that work collaboratively to make our business run. We refer to the people we do business with as "clients" instead of customers, because clients keep coming back month after month, whereas customers are one-and-done. We use the phrase "run the play" when we give our salespeople a specific product or pitch to use as a strategic focus while speaking with clients.

There's a game plan for everything we do. Every team in the Company has a weekly game plan they stick to. They hold daily huddles to review current events and projects. It's all purposeful and strategic.

In sports, the outcome is ultimately dictated by strategy, effort, and mental preparation instead of who is bigger, faster, and stronger. Business works the same way. Regardless of your profession, your success is likely driven more by your preparation and game plan than your actual skill level.

Success doesn't happen accidentally. It happens when you have the right game plan in place, you practice well, and you run the play.

Our team gets to go into the office every day and work hard to be No. 1 in the country, just like we always did in the Michigan State basketball program. We know that to get that win, you have to be great every day.

We could have a record-setting day on a Monday, but if we're not as good on Tuesday, we'll get no business. If you make a mistake, you lose. It's over. You've lost that loan, you've lost that account, and you've lost that future revenue stream. Every day is a new game and you either win or lose.

I've seen how the best leaders and players operate in basketball and I can emulate that here. The goal is the same—trying to be No. 1. That's what I'm passionate about, and that's how I've been able to feel right at home in this "boring" mortgage business.

Fast Break Points

✓ Focus on being a good teammate, no matter your perceived status or leadership level. Stand out with performance, and don't ask anyone to do anything you wouldn't do yourself.

✓ Make a list of company terms and phrases that can and can't be used, and then personally live by them daily.

✓ Go into every day and every meeting with a plan for what you want to accomplish.

✓ Set big goals and keep pursuing them. No matter how much you're down, keep playing until the final whistle.

2

LEADING IN
THE WEEDS

IF YOU'RE ANY KIND OF A SPORTS FAN, CHANCES ARE GOOD
you've attended a college or professional basketball game at
some point. Visualize one of those games and any one of the
many timeouts.

The image you have probably includes the players from
each team heading to their respective benches, where they are
surrounded by the rest of their teammates and handed cups of
water or sports drink and towels.

At the same time, the entire coaching staff is probably in its
own mini huddle, maybe 10 feet away from the players. During
that little coaches meeting, the head coach is being debriefed
by the assistants regarding what plays have been working or the
opponent's offensive and defensive tendencies.

Once the head coach is fully debriefed, the entire staff joins
the players in the bench area—the head coach sitting directly in
front of the five players currently in the game.

After strategies are discussed and plays are drawn up based
on that initial coaches-only meeting, the buzzer sounds and the
game resumes.

That's a typical basketball game visual. Full and media timeouts play out like that almost everywhere, but not at Michigan
State.

The typical timeout—players resting as coaches talk among themselves, then coaches joining the players to review strategy—is actually a big waste of time.

When the players walk off the floor for a Michigan State timeout, Coach Izzo doesn't do that whole charade with his assistants. He dives right in with the players.

He is fully engaged and maximizes his timeouts. He doesn't have to ask questions, get debriefed, or get suggestions from his staff before relaying the message to the players.

That's because Coach Izzo is totally hands-on in collaborative preparation, film study, and game planning. He doesn't sit back and order his assistants to do everything; it's very much an all-hands-on-deck operation, and because Coach Izzo is so involved in film study and understanding every detail of the other team, he has the luxury of collaborating because he *wants* to, not because he *has* to.

Coach Izzo being so in the loop pays great dividends during in-game situations that can be so fast-paced because he's in the best position possible to act and make decisions quickly. In basketball, full timeouts only last 60 seconds and media timeouts generally run 75 to 105 seconds. If he spent the first 30 seconds of that window being debriefed by his assistant coaches on what went wrong, or what the other team is doing, that's critical time that he's not able to communicate and implement strategy directly with his players. By being fully "in the weeds" of the game plan and scouting report, Coach Izzo is better equipped to effectively coach his players and implement strategy in real time.

The business world operates the same way, a concept I refer to as "being in the weeds of your business" as a leader. It refers to leading with an intimate knowledge of your business and of the various elements and activities that your company is made up of.

It's about being an involved, hands-on leader with an incredible command and understanding of your business—and people will respect your vision more because of it.

Gaining market share is about gaining inches, and you can do that by being in the weeds.

You've got to maximize your time and the efficiency with which you communicate your messaging to the entire team. You especially have to make sure directives are being delivered to the people actually doing the work and executing your game plan, not just the "bosses" who will be barking at them from the sidelines.

I'll sit at reception and take calls alongside our team of welcome associates. I'll sit with underwriters and find out what would make their jobs easier. I eat lunch in the cafeteria and always try to sit with someone new—and expect our leaders to do the same.

The same is true for external communications with our clients. Often, when our Company sends a team to work at trade shows, I'll be the only CEO there. I want to meet our clients and prospects in person to learn about their business and discover new ways to help them.

I don't waste any time. I'm always working and finding out what people are up to. That's how I find ideas. If I only have one minute to coach someone on my team, I need all 60 seconds.

How much time do you, as a leader, spend with fellow leaders at your company to discuss corporate strategies and priorities? Comparatively, how much time do they spend relaying those same key points to team members who are on the front lines? How much of that time has to be dedicated to your team leaders getting *you* caught up on various circumstances before you can even begin to think of drawing up a game plan?

That process takes time. Every minute you spend getting up to speed inhibits your company's productivity. The time you waste playing the "telephone game," going over concepts with your leaders instead of delivering the message directly to the people who will be acting on it, could be the difference between winning and losing.

We hold a weekly meeting with sales leaders and over 500 account executives, and I speak at every one to deliver my message directly to the team. I don't need a buffer.

I'm intelligent enough to understand the details and in the weeds enough to speak to the Closing team about its process of making outbound calls and why I think it's important. I might not be physically doing the closing work, but I know what our clients want, and I know what our closers need to reach peak performance. The point is that I understand the role each team plays in the firm's success. I can relate to the challenges that they each face, because I've stood in their shoes and could do that job if I needed to.

A Meeting Shot Clock

People ask me how involved Coach Izzo was in practices. Asking me if he was *at* practices. It blew my mind.

Not only was Coach Izzo at every practice, he was in control of every second of them. Each practice schedule had a very finely coordinated "run of show" that he made sure we stuck to by the minute, and there was no wasted motion, whatsoever. There was a rhythm and a purpose to everything we did. It was like Coach Izzo was the conductor of an orchestra, where everyone was playing a different instrument, and he was the one that brought it all together.

Every second of our two-and-a-half-hour practices was choreographed. There was a clock up on the wall that continuously counted down for each drill and session of practice, and we were hustling non-stop.

We'd do warm-up drills for 11 minutes, do transition offense drills for 12 minutes, and run to the next spot. Then we'd do rebounding drills for 14 minutes, before quickly moving to the next item on the agenda. We'd split into different areas for specific drills—some guys are doing layups on one side, others are shooting free throws at another hoop, and another group is doing catch-and-shoot drills as the managers are hitting them with passes.

That level of meticulous time management has paid great dividends for our business, as well. How much time is wasted in your meetings by off-topic digressions, small talk, and distracted attempts to brainstorm? Probably way too much. You're too busy and time is too valuable to spend sitting in a room talking unnecessarily when you could be working and moving your business forward.

That's why I incorporated a shot clock and some strict speaking guidelines into our senior leadership meetings at United Wholesale Mortgage.

The rules are simple:

- One at a time, leaders from each team speak. They have two minutes to discuss teamwork and communications topics. Teamwork topics are bigger, all-encompassing issues that impact all teams and need to be addressed. An example would be the leaders in training wanting to increase the number of training hours that team members have to meet on a weekly basis. Communications topics are more "FYI" in nature; for instance, if the marketing team is pushing out a video on social media and wants people to check it out and share it.

- Each person has to stand up when speaking. In a room of 50 people, speakers need to project. Standing also helps ensure people are more visible and speak with authority.
- After that, one leader from each team has two minutes to discuss what their team will be prioritizing in the upcoming week. We have someone running a two-minute shot clock to ensure everyone stays on point.
- No one is permitted to speak about past events (unless it pertains to how we can improve). We distribute a packet before the meeting that includes achievements from the past week. Leaders are expected to read it in advance to avoid wasting time discussing the past.
- The last 15 minutes of the 90-minute meeting are reserved for leaders to hold discussions among themselves. That way they don't have to track each other down after the meeting.

Rules like this apply to all our Company meetings, not just the ones involving senior leadership. Every meeting has to have an agenda and action items, in order to keep them moving efficiently and to ensure that they serve a purpose.

Think about how you lead your team or run your company. Are you in the weeds of your business, or are you more of a figurehead leader? If push comes to shove, could you take the lead in delivering a pitch to a new business prospect? Could you jump into a meeting of your IT leaders or legal team and speak knowledgeably in those specific areas?

That concept of being in the weeds of the business is one I've taken to heart ever since my playing and coaching days at Michigan State. I adapted this philosophy to the mortgage business as I resolved to be hands-on and fully engaged. It was invaluable in gaining a strong grasp of each element of the business as I climbed through the ranks.

At one point, I could have been considered the "12th Man" at United Wholesale Mortgage, as I was the 12th person to join the Company, which has since grown to have nearly 4,000 team members. The Company today has over 30 different teams and 300 captains who are leading our success.

Like most 23-year-olds, I didn't know a single thing about mortgages—or business for that matter. Sure, I had a degree in business management, had gained a lot of "real world" skills from my five years in the Michigan State basketball program and had the benefit of a successful business entrepreneur—my father—for a role model. But I was still your typical college graduate, with wide eyes, lofty career aspirations, and the goal of making a name for myself in whatever I set out to do.

There is no doubt that I was driven to succeed and wanted to perform well, but my father also challenged me and made it clear he wasn't planning on just handing everything to me. The message when I came in was, "Look, Mat, you're my son so you'll always have a job here, but what that job is and how far you advance is entirely up to you."

So, I learned the business from the ground up. My first job was essentially grabbing faxes off the fax machine and walking them to underwriters. I was making $18,000 a year—far less, mind you, than I would have made as an assistant basketball coach at Cleveland State University.

But I stuck to the grind because I knew what I wanted, and because I knew this profession, and leading United Wholesale Mortgage was going to be my life. I wanted to learn everything and asked an obscene amount of questions along the way. I knew that if I wanted to be an expert and really understand the ins and outs of mortgages, I had to keep asking questions. I wasn't worried about being a nuisance. I learned how things were done in underwriting and closing. I read guidelines at night. I was an account executive and also originated loans. I made sure I could do a little bit of everything.

Along the way I gained a solid grasp of how the business works. Eventually, I morphed from the basketball guy who knew nothing about mortgages into a mortgage expert.

I wanted to play a big role in leading the Company to new heights and knew I needed to have a general mastery of everything before I would have the credibility to effectively lead others. So, I practiced writing loans on weekends. I worked on one team after another and job shadowed more seasoned people to really learn the ropes of the business.

The mortgage business is incredibly fast-paced and there are a lot of moving parts. Every day we're figuring out what our game plan is, what we're doing with technology, what products the sales team is focusing on, meeting the requirements of a very regulated environment, or different ways to deliver an outstanding client service experience.

But, with everything that happens on a daily basis, there isn't one single thing that I *need* to be briefed on.

Don't get me wrong, I absolutely value the collaboration that can be seen and felt throughout the office. I always want to hear other peoples' ideas, regardless of their status at the Company. But I don't *need* to be briefed. I don't outsource anything.

Of course, I trust the experts at our Company to know what's going on and to develop the best strategies and game plans to move forward, but there's never any doubt that I personally am up to speed with what's going on at the Company and in the industry.

I personally call our clients—something other CEOs might feel is beneath them. But that hands-on approach is how I'm best able to quickly and appropriately impact change.

Sure, I don't *have* to speak to our clients, because we have a team of over 600 account executives that speak to their respective clients every day. Likewise, our clients have access to underwriters, closers, and other support staff, in addition to the aforementioned client service team. There are a lot of client service touch points available to them.

But it makes a difference when the CEO is the person making the call. It shows just how important client feedback is and how much we value the experience they have with us.

Client service is also important internally, and I extend that same level of availability and professional courtesy to our team members.

I make sure that I'm always accessible to my team, like a doctor who is on call. We're a big Company that's always chasing big, aggressive goals, and I've set the bar high for nearly 4,000 other people to work their hardest to reach them. I owe it to them to be in the trenches with them. If I ask an IT team leader to stay 45 minutes after work to make sure a system is up and running so our clients can use it, I stay with them.

Even though I may not have the technical skill set to fix the IT issues, I'm there for support and to help make critical decisions. I'll make phone calls and help out any way I can.

Don't Schedule Anything for Thursday

When I became CEO in 2013, I put "No Meeting Thursdays" into effect. It's insane how quickly my calendar can fill up every week with meetings, phone calls, business lunches, and presentations. While all of those things are necessary to running and growing a business, they can prevent you from really staying engaged on a deeper level. So that's why, for one day a week, I keep my calendar wide open.

Literally nothing can be put on my calendar on Thursdays—not even a phone call with a reporter. The only thing on my agenda for the day is touching base with my people, not only with the executive leaders, but also with other leaders and team members throughout the Company that don't directly report to me.

It's a great opportunity to discuss what's going on and gather ideas and information. These focused one-on-one conversations essentially shape my game plan for the following week.

At the beginning of the day, I'll make a list of peoples' names on a sheet of paper that I want to check in with for specific reasons and carry that around in my pocket all day. Then I make my rounds, checking them off one by one.

No Meeting Thursdays free me up to keep a pulse on the Company's culture and make sure that people are happy with things going on at the Company. Even if a conversation has nothing to do with business, it goes a long way to solidifying the family-oriented culture that I want here.

I even took it a step further and mandated all our captains also implement No Meeting Thursdays once a month. More than 300 other leaders in our Company now abide by it. I tell them to quickly get through their emails on Thursdays and free up the day for conversations and productive work.

We've also adopted a "No Technology in Meetings" rule to make sure we stay as on-topic and time-efficient as possible. Phones, laptops, and tablets are all banned. This way, people are more actively engaged without the distraction of emails and texts.

Now, don't get me wrong—our Company isn't some kind out outdated, archaic operations. We're a tech company. We have over 600 people working in IT and we're constantly on the cutting edge of innovative technology in the mortgage industry. The ban on technology in meetings is about efficiency and avoiding distractions.

Everyone is susceptible to being distracted by an email or some other notification that pops up on their phones. Then, suddenly you're only half as focused and miss something, or don't have the opportunity to share important information of your own. More can be accomplished collectively when everyone in a meeting is fully engaged, instead of a few people only paying 70 percent attention.

To be the most effective, impactful, and credible leader you can be, you've got to know your business inside and out. Be hands-on. Don't just pawn stuff off on the people working for you and rely on them to regurgitate information back to you. If you want to know your business inside and out and be a true leader, read the whole book instead of the CliffsNotes.

Being in the weeds of your business doesn't mean you don't collaborate. It just means that you don't *have to* collaborate to understand what's going on—because you know it. It's a great feeling.

Lunch is a very easy thing to treat productively. Instead of just browsing Twitter or Facebook, sit with someone you don't know. You don't have to talk business; just try to learn about them. Develop a relationship. It will help with overall team chemistry and could ultimately lead to the sharing of ideas, which makes everyone better.

Be like a quarterback and take command of your offense. Think about Peyton Manning, who was one of the most cerebral quarterbacks in the history of the NFL. He not only mastered his offensive playbook but was so tireless and relentless in game preparation that he seemed to know the opposition's defense just as well.

From thorough film study and breaking down numbers, Manning understood defensive tendencies and molded his offensive strategy to take advantage of them.

Apply that mindset of preparation, knowledge, and hands-on capability to how you lead your business. Sit with your IT team members who are developing code for your systems to learn why it is done a certain way. Walk around the office and have one-on-one sessions with various team leaders to stay current with projects that are being discussed and carried out. Do more than just give approval for a final version of a product launch or marketing campaign. Set the criteria up-front for what you want it to look like and stay engaged throughout the process to make sure it's progressing correctly.

Business leaders can really take a lot away from high-performing individuals in athletics. Great leaders in the sports world don't just throw a ball out and have their teams scrimmage on their own. They don't just delegate a bunch of responsibilities to their assistants and coach from afar. They're right there in the action; teaching, implementing, and making sure things are going according to plan.

So, when it comes down to running your business most effectively and maximizing your potential as a leader, be in the weeds. Don't just delegate tasks and pop in with the occasional "Where are we with this?"

Know the progress of your organization's projects and tasks. Be hands-on. Spend time each morning reviewing production from the day before and walk the floors to catch up on things in person. Go to your marketing team and look over the new promotional materials with them so they can explain the direction instead of relying on an email.

Collaboration will always be a valuable part of any success story, and it's important to trust and empower the experts on your team, but there's no excuse for being out of the loop. Don't be a figurehead—be a leader.

Fast Break Points

✓ Schedule fewer meetings. Commit half a day or a full day each week to interacting with your people face-to-face on the floor.

✓ Shadow your team members at every level and meet one-on-one with leaders to discuss timing and status of projects.

✓ Personally call your clients.

✓ In meetings, begin each conversation with, "What can we do to get better?" Give people a time to discuss upcoming items, collaborative opportunities, and ways to improve.

3
FIGHT
AVERAGE

DO YOU KNOW WHAT HAPPENED TO US WHEN WE WERE playing basketball at Michigan State and arrived at one of Coach Izzo's practices a few minutes late?

Trick question.

I couldn't tell you—because it never happened. No one dared to be late to practice.

Over the course of my four-year playing career at Michigan State, we had somewhere around 4,000 practices and workouts. Regardless of what time they were held, we were expected to be there early and ready to go. If practice was at 6:00 AM, we weren't just showing up at 5:50 and casually changing into our practice uniform and shoes. We were expected to show up at least 30 minutes early to get dressed, warmed up, stretched, and work up a light sweat so we were ready to put 100 percent effort into the first drill as the clock struck 6:00.

It was all part of the culture that Coach Izzo created in order to maintain a high level of excellence throughout the program. His expectations eliminated any risk of his team being merely average.

Some people might argue that aiming for average is the safer, possibly even more responsible, route. A low-risk, low-reward move. Sure, you won't make any amazing headlines or capture peoples' attention for something great that you accomplished, but you won't be mocked as a failure either. It's a comfy spot to be in, just coasting through life and meeting the minimum requirements in everything you do. No one can complain about that, right?

But average doesn't win championships. It doesn't land big new clients for your firm or get a feature story on *Good Morning America.*

Average is your worst enemy.

Yet, it's human nature for people to cozy up to it and be content to settle. Being average is just so much easier.

Being average is about doing the bare minimum. You roll out of bed in the morning, eat some breakfast, and get to the office at 8:00 AM, or in my case, often at 5:00 AM. Maybe you're even a few minutes late and blame it on traffic, or on your kids. Then, once you're there, you do the same thing you do every day—exactly what is asked of you and not one thing more. You've been tasked with making 10 phone calls and reviewing 15 case files, and that's precisely what you do. Next thing you know, it's 5:00 PM and you're logging off the computer, walking to your car, and heading home. That's what you do every day, Monday through Friday. That's what your boss expects, so that's what you do.

You're playing it safe. Making sure you check off those boxes on your "job responsibilities" checklist so you can keep bringing home those paychecks. But is that all you want? Do you have any aspirations of advancing, being promoted, or getting a raise? Does the idea of climbing the company ladder mean anything to you?

If the answer is "yes" to any of those questions, you're going about it the wrong way. You're not going to get to the next level and achieve your career goals by being average. That's just not how it works.

There's a Thin Line between Average and Great

Everyone has a line within them, marking the spot where average ends and greatness begins. Ultimately, the difference between the two comes down to your work ethic and attitude. Those two things will always be in your control, regardless of what happens around you.

You can't control if a prospective client returns your call or not, and you can't control things like industry regulations. But you'll always be in charge of your own work ethic and attitude. You wake up every morning and decide if you're going to bring your "A" game or not.

My mindset today is the same as when I was working my way up in the business: I make sure I find one positive thing to take from each day. Even if 99 things go wrong, do whatever it takes to do at least one thing well and mentally make it a great day. Get that one win.

You've got to challenge yourself on a daily basis. If you want to be great at what you do, you have to push yourself accordingly. The decision is yours.

Create a game plan for yourself. Set an ultimate goal that you want to hit five or 10 years down the line, and then be methodical in going after it. Set several mini goals within your game plan that will keep you headed in the right direction.

Sticking to an ambitious plan is a natural deterrent to average behavior.

Back in 2006, I had been working in sales at United Wholesale Mortgage for three years. I was the top producer at the time and had just taken on a leadership role.

This was before our Company was even remotely on the map in terms of being a top wholesale lender. There were only 19 of us working on the wholesale side of the business. We weren't even ranked among the top 200 in the country.

I wasn't used to being so far down in the standings. At Michigan State, we won a national championship and were perennially one of the best basketball teams in the country. I won the President's Award for being the male student-athlete with the highest grade-point average. Now, I was making more loan sales than anyone at the Company.

There was no way I was going to be okay with working for a company that wasn't even one of the top 100, or even 200, in the field. No. That's average thinking, and I was hell-bent on driving our Company to the top.

If I was okay with being part of an average company, I would have settled for just being a friendly local mortgage shop. I wouldn't have worried about being the best and would have just focused on bringing home a paycheck. But that's not how I'm wired, and it's not how I was taught.

I dove in headfirst. I looked for ways our Company could differentiate itself from our competitors.

Right off the top, it started with me. Like a gym rat in basketball, I was the first person to arrive at the office in the morning and the last to leave. Early mornings and late nights were a big part of pushing the Company forward.

I've made it a point to have productive lunches and to entertain clients or team members on evenings and weekends.

One thing I noticed while traveling as an outside account executive was that I missed a lot of opportunities while I was out sitting in other peoples' offices.

At the time, standard practice in mortgage sales—and all business-to-business sales—was essentially to show up at your client's office with a box of donuts and a rate sheet, engage in some small talk, and then repeat the process at each stop along the way. This happened day after day, one mortgage broker office after the next.

And while I was sitting in a broker's office talking about their daughter's volleyball team or their son's guitar lessons, I was missing calls and emails from my other clients who needed my help, whether it was an urgent issue with a loan or an opportunity to close some new business. There was money waiting to be had and I was missing it because I was talking about a broker's weekend plans.

Something had to be fixed. I told my father I wanted to change the way we did business and focus on inside sales. He was understandably a little uneasy about making such a big alteration to our business model and the industry, but he supported my decision and said it was up to me to make sure it worked out.

I decided that going forward, all of our sales discussions would take place over the phone. No more traveling. No more visiting clients' offices. One hundred percent of our sales pitches and business conversations would take place from the comfort of our desks.

It was a groundbreaking move. Everyone in the industry was stuck to the same "boots on the ground" concept for no other reason than that was the way it had always been done.

It took our clients some time to warm up to the change. They were used to speaking face-to-face with their account executive; now they weren't seeing them in person, ever. Initially, some felt the service they were receiving had dipped a bit. Limited to phone conversations, the donuts were gone.

But their attitudes soon shifted. Clients found that when they called their account executive to ask a question, someone actually answered the phone. Voicemails and emails got responses within an hour instead of a day or two. Our brokers were closing loans and going through the process much faster than they were before. They weren't getting to see our faces anymore, but they were making more money and getting their clients into their homes faster—and that's what they really cared about.

As that success became more widespread, we had more of our existing clients send us more of their business, and we had more prospective clients sign up to work with us.

Define What Great Means to You

What makes you a great CEO or leader? Actually define what "great" means to you with measurable goals and then work toward it. Numbers-wise or achievements-wise, based on your profession, what does a great day or great month look like? Define it.

The same concept works in your personal life. If you want to be a better parent, actually define some measurable goals to hold yourself accountable to. If you just generically say, "I want to be a better dad this year," that doesn't necessarily mean anything. There are 100 different things that can mean. But one metric you might hold yourself to, and evaluate yourself on, could be taking each of your children on a one-on-one experience once a month.

Does that mean you're a great dad if you accomplish that goal each month? No. Does it mean that you're a bad dad if you fail to hit the goal one month? No. But it's directionally correct. Measurements matter. If you define what "great" means to you, then you can work toward it.

Set Ambitious Goals, Then Stick to Them

As we started climbing the rankings, I continued sharing my goal of being the No. 1 wholesale lender in the country to anyone who would listen—my family, my close friends, everyone in the office. It was a process that took time, and my goals reflected that. We methodically grew our business at United Wholesale Mortgage, from an "unranked" wholesale mortgage lender to a Top-250 lender. Then I set higher goals and we grew to become a Top-100 lender, then Top-50, then Top-10, and then, ultimately, the No. 1 wholesale lender.

I'd write down my goals on pieces of paper. They were all over the place. I'd occasionally get scolded when little bits of scrap paper were in the laundry because I forgot to empty my pants pockets before putting them in the washer.

Some goals were for specific days or for a week, a month, a year, or even five to 10 years out. When the mortgage market really declined from 2007 to 2010, I kept looking forward, driven to weather the storm and make sure we were in a great position when the market inevitably got stronger again.

Every day, I made sure that I was able to take one small step forward toward my goals. Even on days where it seemed impossible to make progress, I always found something positive to keep us moving forward.

My written goals kept me focused, on our mission, and prevented me from settling for anything remotely similar to average.

Each of us makes a conscious decision every single day to be average or to be great. Look at your own situation. How willing are you to do the little things to be more successful at your job, or other elements of your life? If you're in some kind of sales position, how often do you practice your pitch or practice telling your story? Do you record yourself and then go back and review the game film like athletes do with their practice tape?

It's hard to be great at what you do. At the end of each day, ask yourself, "Did I push myself to be great today?" Well, did you? Because if you didn't, you just wasted a day.

None of us are on this earth forever, so what's the point of letting an entire day go by without trying to be great? In a fast-paced business world, you don't have many days to waste.

There aren't any shortcuts available when it comes to being great, and you've got to be consistent and your efforts need to be ongoing. Bring the same energy and focus in the last 10 minutes of your day that you do first thing in the morning. If you have a list of 20 people you want to call on a particular day and you get through your list with three hours to spare, go for 30. Have real business conversations that add value. Send follow-up emails to people you called yesterday or earlier in the day.

Every company in America starts each year with big aspirations. Everyone comes up with goals and develops a long-term game plan and strategy to achieve those goals. Regardless of how the previous year ended, every company positions itself to gain momentum moving forward, whether that's through strategic hires, the development of new products or programs, or a new marketing campaign.

The goals are primarily the same for every company in every business: grow in size, add more clients or customers, increase market share, and make more money. And they all believe they have the perfect formula in place to succeed.

The same can be said for individuals in the workplace. Each person who works in your field has their own goals, and undoubtedly gets a quick jump out of the gates in January. Average is like the New Year's resolutions that result in a spike in gym membership and attendance that only lasts a few weeks. Greatness is about putting in the work day after day, all year long.

The parallel between business and sports, in this regard, is incredible. Look at professional basketball. Every team that wins the NBA title goes through the same process. After being praised and talked about, paraded around and congratulated for an entire off-season, all the defending champions begin the next season the same way—with a home game where, before the current season gets under way, the team celebrates *last year's* success.

Surrounded by a gigantic amount of fanfare, there is a ceremony in which the players receive their championship rings and witness a championship banner being raised to the rafters. It's a tremendous feel-good moment for the team and the fans alike, but it almost seems like the message is a bit backward. Why make last year's triumph such a focus of the present when you're about to kick off a completely different season?

Now, don't get me wrong. There's nothing wrong with immortalizing a great accomplishment and cherishing its memory forever. I still think about that 2000 NCAA championship victory of ours every day. Believe me when I tell you—I value the everlasting significance of excellence and championships. It's just that the timing of the celebration can make it difficult to stay vigilant in the fight against average.

Each season in the sports world stands alone. Regardless of a team's past success, it always enters each season with a clean slate and the goal of being the best. Winning the championship last year doesn't contribute any extra wins this year. Each fiscal year in the business world stands alone, as well.

You might finish the year ranked as the No. 1 real estate agent in your state, but when the calendar gets flipped over to the next year, everybody starts at zero. You've got nothing to enter the season with, except a nice big target on your back from every other agent in the state who wants to surpass you for the top spot. It's up to you to decide what happens. Do you get comfortable and content, reminiscing about last year's triumph and continually dusting off that trophy? Or do you put your head down, get back to the grind, and work on winning it all again?

That's a challenge I've laid down to everyone who works at my Company. We were the No.1 wholesale mortgage lender in the country in 2015. We did a fun thing with our team members where we had a "National Champions" banner designed and printed, and we hung it in our lobby for everyone to see. We also had a cool trophy created to commemorate the accomplishment—it's a shiny glass material and sculpted into the shape of "1." It's on full display in the middle of our lobby as well.

It was obviously an awesome milestone that was made possible because of everyone's hard work and dedication, but I didn't want that to be it. I didn't want being the No.1 wholesale lender in America in 2015 to be the pinnacle of our Company's success. I wasn't satisfied with that, and I didn't want anyone else in the Company to start resting on their laurels, thinking that we'd "made it," either. So, I laid out the challenge heading into 2016.

I told our team that, not only did I want to be the No. 1 wholesale lender in the country again in 2016, I wanted to be No. 1 by a greater margin. I wanted to widen the gap between us and whatever competitor of ours finished second. I wanted us to be in a league of our own.

Mission accomplished. Our team took that challenge and ran with it. Not only did we repeat our title as the country's best wholesale lender in 2016, we shattered our Company record for annual loan production.

The same challenge was in place for 2017, 2018, 2019, and will continue to be the standard we work toward every year. Our goal is to continue raising the bar. At one point, we focused on doubling the business of whichever competitor of ours finishes the year ranked second. Since then, we had the goal in mind of tripling the business production of the No. 2 company. Now, we have our sights set on becoming the No. 1 overall mortgage company in America—counting both wholesale and retail lenders. All those giant banks that you and your family and friends have savings accounts at, all those mega online lenders you see commercials for—we want to be bigger than all of them.

This mindset is what separates great from average. I'm not ever going to be completely satisfied. We could have the highest market share in the industry at 30 percent—which would be a big deal—but that still means that 70 people out of every 100 do their business with someone else. That's not good enough. It's a huge opportunity for us to continue to grow.

Average isn't allowed in our building. I don't want to be around it. There aren't any shortcuts. If you want to be great at what you do, whether you're a financial advisor, an attorney, or someone running airport operations, you've got to outwork your competition. That's just the mindset I've always had, even from before my basketball playing days at Michigan State, and it's prevalent in all aspects of life.

Honestly, if I can't be the best at something, or see the opportunity to become the best, I don't have that feeling of excitement to do it. There's nothing that I don't see the opportunity to be the best at. And it can be something simple or trivial.

The thing that drives me is the desire to be great, to be No. 1. It's not about money. It's definitely not about fame or recognition. I want to be the best.

What makes you a great CEO or leader? What makes you a great mom or dad? What makes a great husband or wife? Dig deep and find out, and then go after it consistently.

Always push yourself in the fight against average. Find out what you've got inside. If there's a touch of greatness in there and you can bring it to life, how cool would that be?

Fast Break Points

✓ Set a series of measurable goals for yourself—one long-term goal for five to 10 years down the line, and mini milestones at different intervals along the way (weekly, monthly, quarterly, etc.) to keep pace.

✓ Write down your goals and talk about them with people close to you. Make them clear to your team. It'll help you stay accountable to yourself. Don't expect success overnight—focus on taking one step forward every day.

✓ Find something in your business or industry that is done routinely across the board—a process or methodology—and do it differently, and better.

✓ Prioritize training and coaching within your organization. Invest in your people and ensure that everyone is consistently getting better.

CHOOSE SUCCESS

IT'S EASY TO SPOT THE PEOPLE WHO ARE HARD-WIRED TO be successful. They have the personality and mindset that's always "on," even when they don't have to be. It was a trait that was easy to spot in Coach Izzo from the very beginning.

Like March Madness every year, during our 2000 national championship run, the NCAA tournament ran for three weeks. As long as your team keeps winning, you play two games a week. There's barely enough time to catch your breath after one victory before it's time to start preparing for the next opponent. That meant a lot of late nights for our coaching staff, dissecting game film and putting together scouting reports and game plans. In between film sessions, practices, and traveling, there was barely enough time for coaches to sleep, let alone go home and see their families.

That year, the tournament ran from March 16 through April 3. That final Monday was the day we all took turns climbing a ladder with a pair of scissors and cutting off a small piece of the basketball net. And then we all got to lock arms and watch CBS' "One Shining Moment" video, while wearing a championship hat and T-shirt covered in confetti.

We had just beaten the Florida Gators by a score of 89–76 to win the title. The next morning, we were on the bus headed to the airport to fly back to East Lansing, and I couldn't believe what Coach Izzo was doing. He was already talking and strategizing with his coaches on recruits and what we were going to do for off-season workouts.

We had just won the national championship the night before, and he had already put it behind him. Everyone else was still on cloud nine.

Who knows how much he had slept the night before, if at all. But here he was, not basking in his success but back to the grind. He knew that he had ground to make up against other schools in recruiting because, while he and his staff were focusing on our team and our tournament run, other schools could focus all of their attention on talking to high school prospects. Even after winning the national championship, Coach Izzo was hard-wired to be successful. No one was going to outwork him.

I filed that memory away and found myself doing a similar thing years later while leading United Wholesale Mortgage.

It was 2015 and, at the time, we were the No. 2 wholesale lender in the country, on the doorstep of achieving our goal of being No. 1.

Along with about 15 of our leaders, I went to Las Vegas for the annual National Association of Mortgage Brokers Conference, the premier conference in the mortgage industry. It was a Friday-thru-Sunday trip. When we got out there on Friday, we spent the night socializing with some of our clients. It was definitely a long day because we had worked a normal day that Friday and then stayed out until midnight in Las Vegas—which was actually 3:00 AM on our body clocks.

But that next morning, we were all awake, dressed in suits, and ready to go. We were networking, shaking hands, holding meetings, attending seminars, and giving product demos throughout another very long day. And we turned around and did the same thing on Sunday. Everyone that went on that trip packed their "A" game and it showed. I was incredibly proud. It wasn't the same as a two-week-long national championship march in college basketball, but it was about as hard as a group of professionals wearing suits could work in such a tight timeframe.

We took a red-eye and got back to Detroit at 6:00 AM Monday. I called the team together for a huddle around the luggage carousel. It was obvious that everyone was exhausted— and most likely looking forward to using a vacation day to get back to normal.

I looked at them all and said, "Today is why we're going to be the No. 1 wholesale lender in America."

It was as if those "day off thought bubbles" above everyone's heads just vanished. I could practically see them pop.

I reminded them that every other lender in the country was going to use that day for rest and recovery. They were going to be sleeping while we were closing loans. We went into the office that morning, like any other Monday. We were able to get our teams fired up to perform at a high level because we were leading by example.

Everyone was committed to outworking the competition. We chose success that morning, and it catapulted us into becoming the No.1 wholesale lender in the country.

Success Is Up to You

Success is a choice. In the last chapter I talked about refusing to accept average; avoiding complacency and making the leap into greatness. That's a conscious decision all of us have to make individually, and it all comes down to your own work ethic and attitude.

Everything worthwhile in life is earned, and all of us are in control of our own success. I learned from my father early on that I wouldn't be successful at anything unless I worked hard. If it was easy, everyone would be successful.

If you're training for a marathon, it takes very little effort to post inspirational quotes and memes on Facebook and Instagram. Waking up at 6:00 AM on a Saturday to run for three hours before it gets too hot outside is a completely different animal.

My father would challenge me, saying, "Mat, you want to be a college basketball player one day, but did you take 200 practice shots before school today? Did you shoot around after school today? What are you doing to get there?"

He instilled in me the belief that, to be the best, you have to want it more than everyone else and you have to make sacrifices. Sometimes you have to give up some sleep or take a night off from binge-watching Netflix to finish a presentation on time. That's just how it works.

When I first started at United Wholesale Mortgage, I didn't know anything about mortgages, but I was committed to learning and becoming great. Instead of just relaxing over the weekends, I'd go to the office to work on writing loans and learning the business by reading guidelines and reviewing our processes.

The picture of where the Company is today compared to when I first started is night and day. We were working out of one room that was about 1,200 square feet. We went on to "upgrade" by expanding into a vacant grocery store, where we had people underwriting loans in what used to be the frozen foods aisle.

My office at the time was essentially a broom closet. There weren't any windows and I had to walk in, turn around, and shut the door so I had enough space to sit down.

Now we're working out of a beautiful headquarters that is over 600,000 square feet—with tons of windows and open space everywhere.

Focus on the WIN—What's Important Now

Attitude is another thing that is learned. Negativity has seemingly become the norm in our society. Similarly, it has become more normal to *not* have a great work ethic. But those are both learned traits.

The biggest thing for me while growing up was learning that attitude and work ethic dictate success and that you can choose to be good in those areas. It's completely up to you. It was a simple equation for me to figure out and apply to my life: if I wanted to succeed, and success is dictated by a great work ethic and a great attitude, then I was going to demonstrate those things.

When you set goals, focus on the WIN—What's Important Now. You have to understand that success doesn't happen overnight. Take it one day at a time and achieve one little win each day. Get the business card of a decision-maker. Connect with one person on the phone who had never taken your call before.

Focus on getting that one accomplishment each day that creates progress in the right direction. Then repeat the process on a daily basis until it becomes routine. Don't get down if you make a mistake or get into a rut. Just be positive and work harder. Bounce back.

The great thing about being part of a team is that a strong work ethic has a snowball effect. Everyone feeds off one another. One by one, it grows. Everyone continues working harder and pushing each other. That's how you have a great team. Suddenly, you have an entire team arriving early to a practice or a workout to get some extra shots in.

When I was first learning the ropes as an account executive, I went to the office on weekends to make calls and put in extra time to acquaint myself with our clients' business. I researched clients' backgrounds, so I could do a better job of building rapport as part of the selling process. By doing so, a few other people took notice and started doing the same thing. It didn't just help us, it helped the Company get better.

Our team at Michigan State didn't get to the gym at 6:00 AM to take shots because Coach Izzo told us to. We all did it because guys like Mateen Cleaves and Jason Richardson went in at 6:00 AM and told us to join them. Everyone was doing it together, trying to push each other, and that great work ethic became contagious.

You didn't hear guys complaining about playing time. The only thing that mattered was that we won the game. I remember games where Mateen had a bad shooting night and only scored three points, and he was the happiest guy in the locker room after the game. A lot of people that don't carry themselves with a positive, team-first attitude would be sulking in that situation.

As an individual, I came to value a positive attitude and strong work ethic when I realized that everyone else didn't have them. I started to really focus on basketball when I was eight years old because I had goals of playing at a higher level. I spent time dribbling the basketball outside in the driveway, really working at it. There were times when I chose not to meet up with my buddies for ice cream because I hadn't taken my 200 shots yet.

When I was playing in actual games, I was diving headfirst for loose balls. I was putting it all out there and, looking around, noticed that no one else was hustling like me. I was shocked. That is something they can control, and they just weren't doing it. That gave me my in.

I've never had unbelievable athletic ability and am quite willing to admit that I can't dunk. But I've had the work ethic and attitude that other people can emulate but choose not to.

It got me excited because, when I realized that other people weren't diving for loose balls and people weren't willing to come in early or stay after practice, I understood that I *could* play basketball at Michigan State. I knew I could outwork people. It was all about heart. Other players might have had more skill and natural talent than me, but they didn't have the same drive and work ethic to play at a place like Michigan State, so I knew I could get there, myself.

It's that belief and determination, and ultimately your choice to take the first steps toward pursuing success, that will dictate how much you accomplish. And there's no question that you will face obstacles along the way. Your boss might shoot down a great idea. A colleague might throw you under the bus during a meeting. A client might leave you for a competitor. That's business. That's life. But you can't let negative things prevent you from reaching the level of success that you aspire to achieve.

One question that I pose to our team members all the time is, "Are your work habits today on par with the dreams that you have for tomorrow?"

Asking yourself that question every day becomes an incredibly powerful motivator. It's very to-the-point and easy to put into action. If you dream of achieving a certain level of success in anything you do, every action you take—or don't take—on a daily basis will dictate whether you achieve it or not. If you want more, you have to do more. Everything you've done to this point has gotten you to where you currently are. If you're comfortable where you're at, keep doing what you're doing. But if you want more, if you want to advance in your profession or build your business, you have step it up in terms of effort, creative thinking, relationship-building, or practicing your craft, whatever it might be.

If you want to be the top underwriter at your company, are you showing up early and staying late? Are you getting through five more loan files a day than you have to? Putting in extra work over the weekend to stay organized and be ready to go during the week? When it's all said and done, looking at your daily efforts in comparison to your end goal, are you really giving it your all?

It goes back to consistency being key. Every day, every week, and every month is about making progress. Moving forward. Putting forth the effort needed to achieve a dream isn't a one-day thing or something for "when you get around to it." You've always got to be on.

You might have an off day here and there, performance-wise, but your work ethic can never afford to miss a day. There will be some days that no one answers or returns a single one of your phone calls. It happens to everyone. But don't ever sacrifice the hustle and the grit for the next day or opportunity.

If you're a leader within your company, it's crucial that you convey that message to your team members as strongly as possible. You can even be creative about it.

We had one of the nation's top motivational speakers, Eric Thomas, come into our headquarters to talk to our team members. He had become famous in his field for introducing the concept of, "When you want to succeed as bad as you want to breathe, then you'll be successful."

Eric is a living, breathing example of "choosing success." Before becoming a well-known and high-earning speaker, he was a high school dropout and lived homeless on the streets of Detroit for over two years.

He continues to rewrite his history every day, adding new chapters to his legacy all the time. He went back to school and eventually went on to college, where it took him 12 years to get a four-year degree.

Why is that fact relevant? It doesn't matter how long it took to get there. A degree or a diploma doesn't list how long it took you to achieve it. The only date it shows is the date it was received. Eric Thomas earning his degree after more than a decade was no different than someone else earning it ahead of schedule, in three years.

Success is success. It doesn't have an expiration date. I say it all the time—I don't care about peoples' résumés. I'm not interested in their credentials or achievements from other companies. It doesn't matter to me if someone went to one of the best schools in America like Harvard or Yale.

All I care about is what someone does here. If you want to be successful and get promoted at this Company, show me that you're the best. Be the obvious choice.

It might be a little of that walk-on mentality showing through in my leadership, but I believe everyone gets what they work for. I walked on at Michigan State as someone who averaged 23 points per game and was a top high school basketball player. But it didn't matter. I had to show on the court that I could play at the college level—the Michigan State level.

Someone's past accolades, or the level they had risen to at another company, doesn't necessarily dictate their role at United Wholesale Mortgage. If you had been a Vice President of Sales somewhere else, you could start out as an account executive here. Prove that you're a high performer and you can climb to team leader and then division leader and then reach vice president of sales.

Three of our Company's C-level leaders—our chief operating officer, chief people officer, and chief digital officer—all started at United Wholesale Mortgage at more entry level roles, in underwriting, marketing, and sales, respectively.

Each demonstrated advanced knowledge and leadership traits in their specific areas and brought great ideas and implementations to the table. Each person proved themselves as the obvious choice to be elevated into a leadership position. Those success stories, as "homegrown" talent who developed and were promoted from within, mean more to me than if I had just gone out and hired away executives from competitors in the mortgage space.

Success is attainable for everyone; you just have to make the conscious decision to pursue it every single day. No shortcuts are allowed. You can't go into your office and give 100 percent effort on Monday and Tuesday, then give 70 percent effort on Wednesday, 50 percent effort on Thursday, and 40 percent effort on Friday, and expect to achieve your goals. Your effort at 5:50 PM on a Friday should be the same as it is at 10:30 AM on a Tuesday.

To be successful, you have to give 100 percent effort every single time you walk into the building and push yourself even when you're not there. You decide exactly how successful you become.

Fast Break Points

✓ Align your work habits of today with your dreams for tomorrow.

✓ Be productive in those small pockets of time that present themselves throughout the day. Eight minutes before a meeting? Don't just browse social media. Do prep work. Research. Get a head start on your task that you're going to tackle right after the meeting. Gain every inch you can.

✓ Focus on the WIN ("What's Important Now") when setting goals, and make sure you earn little victories every day. You don't have to achieve a big goal in one day, but make sure that each day is a step in the right direction.

5
CULTURE
IS KING

IF I WERE TO ASK YOU TO LIST THE COUNTRY'S MOST successful men's college basketball programs of all time, what would you say?

You'd probably give me the same names that everybody else would: Duke, UCLA, Kentucky, Michigan State, North Carolina, and Kansas. And it probably took you less than three seconds to spit those names out.

Those schools are in that upper-echelon, elite tier when it comes to basketball. They're recognized as the "blue bloods" of the sport. That nickname comes from that fact that these programs are steeped in tradition and have had storied, long-term success in the game. They've been around forever, have always won a lot of games and championships, and are always in the discussion to win even more. The names on the front of the jerseys essentially do all the marketing and recruiting for the programs on their own.

What's the main reason the blue bloods have enjoyed such sustained success over the years? It's because they've been able to carry themselves for a long time as programs where winning is part of their culture. Excellence is an expectation in these programs.

A lot of it comes down to a sense of tradition and the belief that the name on the front of the jersey is more important than the name on the back of the jersey.

Current players at the University of North Carolina know they're putting on the same jersey that Michael Jordan wore. When I was at Michigan State, I was wearing the same green-and-white uniform that Magic Johnson donned for two years. It's that kind of feeling that propels you to always bring your "A" game and deliver excellence on a daily basis, because the people before you set that tone.

Programs are born by developing a culture that lays the foundation for long-term success. You've got to create an environment where core beliefs and principles are known and upheld, where individuals adhere to a system, and where strategic vision accounts for long-term sustainability instead of setting for short-term success. A program is a place where winning is engrained into the DNA of your organization; it's expected, not just desired.

Switch over to the business world and the same kind of concepts are at work. Culture is king if your company is going to achieve long-term sustained success, both as a workplace and on the bottom line.

Culture will always play the central role in building a successful program that wins with consistency. When you create a culture of winning, winning just happens. Just like any successful team, your company needs to have a winning culture, a disciplined culture, if you want to be great.

Culture Eats Strategy for Breakfast

The creation and execution of an overall strategy is critical for meeting objectives of a long-term plan, and it's an important-sounding topic to discuss in senior leadership meetings. But the reality is that your culture determines how well your strategies get implemented, if at all.

It doesn't matter how innovative your technology is or how perfectly your client service model is set up. If your culture isn't built to satisfy and motivate your people, your business won't succeed as well as it should.

People need to feel comfortable sharing their opinions. There needs to be a sense of transparency in how and why decisions are made, and there needs to be an understanding that your team can have a say in the decisions their leader makes. Getting your team to buy in to the program is a big deal.

Culture impacts how many deals your sales team makes or how many new clients your business development team sign up. Culture plays a role in how friendly your external-facing team members are when they interact with clients. Your company's ability to retain talent, develop peoples' skills, and keep people engaged in their work are determined by culture.

The team with the best players usually wins, so we follow a pretty simple formula to make sure we have the best players: we recruit the best people to join the Company, train them up so they can be the best version of themselves, and then treat them so well that they never want to leave.

In order for our Company's culture to thrive as a team, I place a lot of value in three things:

1. **Work-life balance.**
   Here, we live by a philosophy we call "Firm 40." It's our way of saying come in and grind for eight hours a day, and then get out of here and go be with your family and friends.

   The "Firm" part of "Firm 40" is on our team members, and the "40" part is on leadership.

We don't live to work, we work to live. Sure, people can put in 60 to 70 hours of work in a week, but that's not sustainable long-term. You will burn out at some point.

But similar to a college basketball coach pushing his or her players to give maximum effort for the full 40 minutes of a game, we push our team members to give a full 40 hours of focused, productive work each week.

Team members grind for eight hours a day, with a one-hour lunch mixed in for a mental break, sort of like a halftime intermission. It might not take a full hour to eat lunch, but take 20 or 30 minutes to eat and then run errands, go for a walk, get your mind right. Then come back refreshed and ready to dominate in the second half of the day.

Instead of using the last five minutes on a Friday to start a group text with friends about plans for that night, I want our team members staying focused and proactive. Pull up the next file and do some research on the client. Write down some notes on them so it's easy to hit the ground running on Monday morning.

2. **Camaraderie among team members.**
My biggest pet peeve at the Company is if two people are walking toward each other in a hallway and they don't look up at each other, don't smile, and don't say hello. I can't stand that.

Someone might say, "Mat, it's just not my personality." And I (jokingly) tell them to change their personality. Be friendly to people. You don't have to go out and grab drinks with them. Just be nice. That's what we do here.

We have a huge cafeteria with a lot of big tables. I go down there all the time and sit down with new people. I use it as an opportunity to learn more about what different people do here. More importantly, I find out what their interests and hobbies are outside of work.

I do the same thing when we take a group of 25 raffle winners on a day trip to Cedar Point, a popular amusement park a couple hours away in Sandusky, Ohio. The trip is about getting away and having fun, but I use the two-hour bus ride to and from the park to sit with people and get their opinions on certain projects or how our Company can improve.

It's not a process that's limited to me. All of our team members are encouraged to shadow people on other teams for 30 minutes every so often. The results are two-fold: it helps everyone gain a well-rounded understanding of how the different teams help our Company function, and it invites a fresh outsider perspective for idea-sharing.

Not everything needs to be work-related, either. I tell our leaders to support initiatives that other teams are doing. If another team is hosting a bake sale to raise money for a special cause, go check it out. You want people to support you when you have something going on. Inside, we all want to feel that support and have other people show an interest in what we're doing.

3. Make it a place you're proud of.

I want our Company to be a place that our team members are proud to have their families and friends visit—or work. We have a headquarters that we're really proud of, so we encourage our team members to give a quick tour to anyone they bring in to the office.

We hold events every year that make working at our Company a unique and memorable experience. Some allow our team members to bring in their families to integrate with their work family.

There's a Company fair where all our team members bring their families out for an evening of unlimited rides and free food, drinks, and games.

Every Halloween, we let our team members decorate our building with a bunch of different themes and invite our team members' families to come in and trick-or-treat with their kids.

We go all out for our big end-of-year holiday parties, where we'll have great food and bring in big-name performers to entertain our team members with surprise on-stage mini concerts.

We have Company-wide raffle drawings at the end of each year where team members win a cruise to the Bahamas for themselves and a guest.

More Than Perks

The list of examples of the fun things we do here goes on and on, but culture can also be built into the way you do business on a daily basis.

We decided to do away with internal email and replaced it with an enterprise-wide communications platform that we named UZone.

UZone is all-inclusive: it serves a task-based project management system, a Twitter-like communications timeline, library for Company resources and information, and so on. Not including communications with external clients, our team members can function completely within UZone.

There was a time when we used to send an email out seemingly every 40 minutes about things that were going on at the

Company, or we used huge group emails to communicate about projects. That's ancient history.

Now, UZone tasks are simple. You want me to do something for you? Assign me a task and give me a deadline and a description of what you're looking for. If it's a group project and we need several people to contribute multiple different things, you can assign tasks to as many people as you want within the specific project. Specific comments don't get accidentally buried or skimmed over in an email thread.

On top of that, it's an avenue for people to have fun. Team members can share funny pictures or post jokes or other engaging content. It truly connects our entire Company in a way that didn't exist before UZone was created. That impact, itself, has taken our culture to new heights.

Be Accessible

It makes a big difference when team members feel that their CEO, or their leader, is hands-on and is interested in how they're functioning in their day-to-day roles.

I regularly shadow people on different teams throughout the Company to experience the business firsthand from their vantage point.

One time in particular, I sat with one of our newer account executives on the sales floor to hear how his conversations went with his mortgage broker clients.

From speaking with him and getting his thoughts on the sales techniques that we coach our people to execute, I was able to go back to our sales leadership team and implement more focused training sessions for people who had been on the sales floor for less than a year, better preparing them to respond to objections.

Recognize People's Effort

I make it a point to let our team members know that the effort they give is appreciated and doesn't go unnoticed. Every week, during our sales meeting, I read names of individuals who achieved "perfect weeks" and "perfect months," which are effort-based metrics based on different criteria such as the number of focused business conversations they have over the phone and the percentage of their incoming calls that are answered instead of going to voicemail.

In addition to reading off the names of these honorees and having them stand in front of 500 of their peers, "perfect month" winners receive a special card that gives them month-long access to an exclusive VIP room, where they can enjoy an array of snacks, candy, beverages, and entertainment.

I also like to personally recognize team members' achievements. Every morning, I view reports that provide status updates for IT projects we have going on, underwriting quality, and other operational numbers to see who some standout performers are throughout the Company. I don't compare people against their peers to see who is excelling, I look for people who are surpassing their usual output. Then I leave voicemails to let them know I'm proud of them.

Leaving a "job well done" voicemail is so simple. It doesn't take any longer than 15 seconds, and then you continue down your to-do list. But from the perspective of the team member who receives that voicemail, it's a big deal. The CEO actually noticed your hard work and took the time to give you a personal shout-out.

One time, a group of 12 people on our IT team had spent several months developing a new technology and, when we successfully launched the product, I called all the developers and business analysts associated with the project personally to congratulate them on a job well done. I told them to be proud because they had effectively changed the mortgage industry for the future.

They were quick calls, no more than 30 seconds each. Making those calls to 12 people only took me six minutes. That's not a lot of time, but it made a huge impact on them.

One person, in particular, felt on top of the world. He told his team leader that he had never been that excited to get back to work on the next big revolutionary project. He went home that evening and told his wife about it, and she started crying because she was so happy for him.

After people get recognition like that, they're fired up to smash the day. Let people know the impact they're making. Hit them with a couple compliments, and they're ready to fly.

Culture Starts at the Top

Leadership matters. Leaders build the culture, culture shapes work ethic, and work ethic produces results. When you, as a leader, embody the culture, communicate it effectively through words and actions, and then build trust with your people, that alignment is a strong driver of performance.

People follow their leader first, and the vision second. Training your people on leadership, or how to do something, isn't effective and won't ignite any change unless the leaders of your company get that same training first.

There needs to be clear cohesion and buy-in throughout your organization. It takes a complete team effort, from the CEO down to interns. Everyone is on one team, working together to accomplish a shared goal.

There isn't an off-season when it comes to building a culture. You and your team always have to be "on" if you want to be a winning program. You have to lead every day and build culture every day to reinforce it. As you bring people on board, you have to integrate them quickly so they can get up to speed and committed to how the cycle of performance works.

When you establish a company culture where success is expected and characteristics like a strong work ethic and attitude are required, you position your business to succeed over the long haul. In a fast-paced business world that is full of competition, that's how you'll brand your company as a winning program that stands the test of time.

Fast Break Points

✓ Focus on creating a strong culture, not just a strong business plan. Do things that make your people feel a sense of enjoyment and pride in their work.

✓ If your budget allows, adopt a project management platform instead of relying on email for all your internal communications. It'll increase communication and collaboration—and be much less of a headache.

✓ Commit to making two phone calls a week to recognize a team member for their hard work or achievements. Especially in a larger company, nothing fires people up more than knowing that they're being noticed by the leader.

EMPHASIZE
THE WHY

YOU WANT TO KNOW WHAT THE MOST HORRIBLE THING IN *the world is when you're a 20-year-old college student?* Waking up early.

As in, waking up early enough to make the sun seem lazy because it's not rising for another couple hours.

Waking up early, even during the summer months, was pretty much all we knew as Michigan State basketball players, and it wasn't the most fun experience. We couldn't understand why Coach Izzo made us do it.

Anyone that played basketball at Michigan State made a major time commitment, and a lot of that time occurred in the wee hours of the morning. We could tell that Coach Izzo drew up the schedule that way on purpose, but we could never figure out why. And he never told us why, either.

Because he didn't have to.

When you're 18 or 21 years old and playing for your school's basketball team, you just do what the coach tells you to do, no questions asked.

If Coach Izzo tells you to run, your follow-up question should be "How fast?" or "How far?" Never "Why?"

If Coach Izzo tells you that you're late when you get to the gym at 5:13 AM for a 5:15 AM practice, you don't question it. You just get to work and make sure you show up by 4:55 AM from that moment on. That's just not how it goes in the coach-player relationship.

Luckily for me, I went on to be a student assistant coach on Coach Izzo's staff during my fifth year. Instead of simply being told what to do all the time, without any explanation behind it, I was in his exclusive inner circle that granted access to the "why" behind his decision-making.

Suddenly everything made sense. He had three very specific reasons for scheduling 5:15 AM workouts in the middle of summer:

1. **Coach Izzo knew that we wouldn't be out late the night before doing anything stupid.**

   One of the things that college coaches fear most is the possibility of his or her student-athletes doing something negative that jeopardizes themselves and puts a black eye on the program or university.

   Scheduling practice for 5:15 AM solved that problem. No one was out late making bad decisions because we were more concerned with getting sleep.

2. **It created additional team building and bonding opportunities for players.**

   Our 5:15 AM workout sessions would end at 6:45 AM. Summer classes began at 8:00 AM. That gave us an hour to eat breakfast, and because timing was so tight, we naturally chose to eat together in the cafeteria. That naturally led to us building camaraderie every day.

   Championships aren't necessarily won by talent alone. A lot of times it comes down to the chemistry you have in the locker room, and those cleverly forced team breakfasts built that chemistry.

3. **It gave us a mental edge.**
   All of us knew that no one else in the country was outworking us at 5:15 AM. So, when it came time to compete against these other teams, we had the mental edge. Another team might be more skilled than us, but they were never going to outwork us or be tougher than us.

   Even outside of off-season training, our practices during the season were so intense that, when game time rolled around, it almost felt like we were getting a break. We worked so hard and prepared so much every day that our attitude was sort of like, "Great, we have a game tomorrow. Thank god we don't have another practice!"

   It's amazing how those reasons make so much sense once you've matured and are given the "why" behind them.

   The same principle applies to the business world. Having been in both situations, it has been a no-brainer for me to lead my Company with that kind of openness and transparency with our people, because I know how much of a difference it makes.

   As decisions are made at our Company, and various goals and strategies are implemented, I always tell everybody why we do everything, and I encourage the other leaders in our Company to do the same.

The Why Creates Clarity

Right off the top, I made sure that everyone at our Company knew why I made the strategic decision I made in how we run our business as a whole.

United Wholesale Mortgage is a business-to-business (B2B) company, which means that we don't serve the end consumers directly. That's different than other mortgage companies you see commercials for all the time. Those are retail mortgage lenders that operate under the business-to-consumer (B2C) model.

My thought process was that, in order for our Company to grow the way I envisioned and to one day become the No. 1 overall mortgage lender in the country, it made more sense to be *great* at one thing as opposed to being *just good* at multiple things.

By focusing 100 percent of our business on wholesale, we've dominated in market share and have grown our loan production every year, even during years where the overall market declines.

It's important to deliver the "why" because it gives validation and reason for the decisions you make—something that's incredibly valuable for leaders to deliver.

Don't Be a Suck-Up

There are two answers that I will never accept at the Company when a leader is asked why we do something a particular way:

"That's the way we've always done it."

"Because Mat wants it that way."

Those are both awful reasons. They're lazy and a complete cop-out. If you're in a leadership role, responsible for guiding a team of people to accomplish specific tasks or goals, you owe it to them to support your directives with legitimate rationale.

If someone is going to go that route, it has to be, "Mat wants it that way *for these specific reasons*. Do you agree or not?"

There has to be a "why" for every decision that is made at each level of an organization to make sure that everyone is on the same page.

I tell our team members that they can challenge me on anything, and I really mean that. If they disagree with me on something or don't understand how or why I made a certain decision, I want them to let me know. I will always be transparent with them. There is never any hidden reason or agenda with the decisions I make, and they really appreciate that.

The focus that we've put on "explaining the why" is how our Company has become so great. We might have been doing something a certain way for a long time and for no real reason. If someone calls me out on it and says it doesn't make sense, we make changes right away.

Coach People Differently

Not everyone is the same. People have different factors that motivate them, different goals that drive them, different styles or preferred ways of doing things. As the leader of a business, or of a team, you have to understand that and put in the time to really get to know your people, and then take an individualized approach to lead each person to their fullest potential.

There isn't a "One Size Fits All" category for leading a group of individuals. You can't coach everyone the same, communicate to everyone in the same manner, and use the same motivational or reward tactics across the board.

If you're a basketball coach, you have to know which players get a fire lit under them and take their game to another level after they are publicly challenged, and which players tend to pout and shut down a bit when they get called out—and then communicate with them accordingly.

When leading a team in the workplace, you'll have some people who take a lot of satisfaction from being publicly recognized for their hard work and accomplishments, while others aren't comfortable, or are indifferent, toward needing that kind of praise. Some people are more driven by things like title or the opportunity to lead people, while others prioritize being in a position where they can be creative and are consistently challenged with new things.

People are different, so coach them differently.

Making Mistakes Is Okay, Just Fix Them Fast

One of our main Company values is "Continuous improvement is essential for long-term success." That's really just a long-winded way of saying, "Change...and change fast." We change all the time here, and while I'm in the weeds of everything that goes on, I'm not an expert on everything. I can't tell you with certainty what the next big piece of technology should be, or how it should be designed.

But if someone on my team says that we should go a certain way, and it makes sense, we try it. I'm not ultimately married to that decision. If it doesn't work as we planned, we can always change it back or adapt it to the next thing.

We're a fast-moving business and always trying new things. A lot of people stick by the adage, "Measure 10 times and cut once," in reference to meticulously planning something out before getting started. I measure once and then I cut once. If it turns out that we made the wrong cut, we'll change it and give it another shot. I'm a believer in trial by error.

Through all of that—the innovation and the change and constant strategizing—the backbone of it all is that level of transparency. The "why" behind it all.

When you equip your office and your team with the green light to challenge you on your decision-making, it not only keeps you sharp and accountable, it works the other way, too. It creates an environment where you're more able to assign projects, provide instruction, and critique peoples' work, because they know it's a two-way street.

There is incredible upside to creating a culture where giving reasons for decisions is an expectation and a responsibility. Whether you're helping millennials stay focused on the task at hand or guiding your company's implementation of a multi-million-dollar mobile app, there's no question that delivering the "why" will take your business to another level.

Fast Break Points

✓ Give your team the "why" behind your decisions, opinions, and strategy. Likewise, encourage your team to always challenge the "why."

✓ Ban people from using the phrases, "That's the way we've always done it," and "Because the CEO wants it that way."

✓ Don't spend too much time planning. Make a decision and go for it. Make necessary changes along the way.

7
MORE THAN RESULTS

THE MOST SUCCESSFUL AND RENOWNED COACHES IN *college basketball all have the same kind of things in common:* an impressive win-loss record, national championship rings, conference championship rings. Some of them might even have a "Coach of the Year" honor or two under their belts.

Some coaches have been immortalized at their respective schools by having the basketball court or part of the arena named after them. Michigan State's student section in the Breslin Center is known as "The Izzone." The Duke Blue Devils play on Coach K Court. Both the University of Tennessee's men's and women's basketball teams play on a court nicknamed "The Summitt" after the late legendary women's coach, Pat Summitt.

Those are probably the achievements that are at the top of your mind when considering what makes a particular coach elite. It's easy to use those baseline metrics to compare one person to another in order to measure their success. That's because the concept behind sports is simple: a team either wins or it loses. It becomes a champion, or it doesn't. It's really cut and dry, black and white. It's a results-based business.

But there's more to it than that.

Coaches always receive credit for helping their players win awards and developing them enough to play professionally, but often the most important development takes place behind the scenes.

Coach Izzo has won a national championship and led several teams to Big Ten championships and appearances in the Final Four. He was inducted into the Naismith Basketball Hall of Fame in 2016.

But if you asked him what his most cherished memories are with his former players, he'd undoubtedly point to the lasting relationships he's built with all of his players and the tight-knit family culture he has built at Michigan State.

He'd take the most pride in bringing guys into his program as 17- or 18-year-old kids and helping them develop into men with character. Teaching them important values like being a good husband and father and teaching them to be responsible people.

The most meaningful thing for him is that, when you come into the Michigan State basketball program, you become part of the family. And you're family forever.

He has instilled a culture where Spartan basketball alumni stay connected to each other and to the program. I know of players who came to Michigan State and later transferred out of the program, but still come back to our reunions, and Coach Izzo welcomes them with open arms. We're a family.

Coach Izzo cares about you, and it's not just for the years that you're playing on the team. You could call him up 10 years down the line, and even though there's nothing you can do to help him at that point, he's still there for you.

Now, don't get me wrong. He's an intense coach and holds everyone highly accountable. Any casual observer of a Michigan State basketball game will notice that. But that's because he so badly wanted us to be successful.

You might see him get upset with one of his players who is walking back to the bench after giving up an easy layup on defense. That's just how he is. But with Coach Izzo, we all knew that he didn't mean anything against us personally when he got upset on the sidelines. It was him passionately doing the job he loves, and it worked because we knew he cared so much about us as people.

Coach Izzo was great at building relationships with everyone off the court. He took the time to break things down to where it wasn't just about basketball and what you were doing on the court. It wasn't just a matter of, "Hey, you come play basketball for me and the rest of it's on you."

He really tried to find out what was going on in your life. There were countless times that he would sit down with guys on the team to help them through different situations, whether it was a girlfriend breaking up with someone, an issue with roommates, or something going on in their families.

He cared about those things. He wanted to know how everyone was doing in class and if you were struggling in a certain class, he'd talk to you about that.

He took the time to understand what was important to his players. Maurice Ager, who was a freshman on the team when I was a student assistant coach, was very religious and going to church was a priority for him. So, on Sundays, Coach Izzo made sure that practices were never scheduled for a time that would conflict with his religious practices.

He respected what was important to us from a personal standpoint, whether it was religion, family visiting from out of town, or making sure we got home for holidays like Thanksgiving. He was very aware of family and that we were human beings, not just basketball players. And because we knew that about him, we reciprocated and were very willing to give our best effort.

Know What Motivates Your People

If you only view your responsibilities as a leader through the lens of motivating your team to hit company goals, you're only doing half your job.

Truly positive and impactful leadership is about more than producing bottom-line business results. When Coach Izzo talks to recruits about playing at Michigan State, he doesn't limit his pitch to his career won-loss record, or even how many Big Ten championships the program has won during his tenure in East Lansing.

He also highlights how many of his former players have been drafted into the NBA, how many of those guys were lottery picks, and how many of his players are developed enough to be high-impact professional players early in their careers.

Those points have to be part of his recruiting pitch because, even though one of Coach Izzo's top priorities is putting a winning basketball team on the floor every year, he understands that playing in the NBA is a goal that his players and potential recruits have. They want to develop their skills and be given an opportunity to showcase their abilities to NBA scouts.

Similarly, a leader in the business world is evaluated based on their ability to develop and prepare the people on their team to reach the next level of their careers.

You can't be a successful long-term business if you're only looking at the business results and you're not looking at the people and what matters to them. If you don't cater to your people and you just push them for results, you'll get results for a month, a quarter, or a couple years, but then they're going to be gone and you have to start over again.

It's also your job to get to know the people on your team and to learn what makes them tick. Find out what their aspirations are and help them get there. If an entry-level person on your staff wants to be a vice president one day, assign him or her tasks, provide training, mentor them, and send them to workshops and seminars that prepare them and put them on that track.

Take a deeper look at your organization. At the surface level, your company is a group of people working together to achieve a common goal, whether that's to be a market leader in unit sales or to be a top revenue producer. But digging deeper, your company is a group of individuals who come to work every day and put forth their best effort to achieve goals.

Why do they do that? What's their motivation to work hard?

You'd be naive to think that all your team members care as passionately about achieving the company goals as you do as the CEO. Their motivation for busting their tails likely isn't because they so badly want to help the company achieve a certain milestone; it's likely because they want that accomplishment to lead to a promotion. Everyone wants to do whatever is necessary to grow and achieve their own goals.

Everyone has a vision and goals for themselves that are separate and apart from the role they play in the greater team construct of your organization. You have to realize that and respect that. Because whether someone chooses to advance their talent at your company or at a different one, it's up to you, as a leader, to make them feel valued and to buy in to their development.

Know Your Role as a Leader

As the leader of a company, it's not my job to make the people at my Company stay up at night, thinking about how many billions of dollars of loan volume that we produce.

My job is to create an environment where they like coming to work every day; where they feel inspired, driven, and challenged. My job is to equip them with the resources they need to do their jobs well, and a culture and an individual attention that makes them *want* to stay at this Company for a long time.

At the end of the day, basic leadership principles are the same no matter the size of your company and team, or what industry you work in.

Your team is more concerned with your credibility of character than your credibility of expertise. People won't buy in to the strategy or the culture if they don't buy in to the leader. Never lose sight of the axiom that your team won't care how much you know until they know how much you care.

Your ability to push and motivate people correlates with the level of trust you've built with them. If your team views you as a self-centered and agenda-driven dictator who chases your own accolades through their hard work, you've already struck out.

Your credibility of character, and the level of trust they have in you, will be so low that it won't matter how knowledgeable you are in the field. You won't be able to motivate them because they won't believe in you. Building their trust in you is critical.

Trust is earned through your actions—by what you say and do on a daily basis.

Here are some actionable steps you can take to strengthen the level of trust that your team has in you:

- **Empower your team.** Allow your people to put their creativity, critical thinking, and other special abilities to use.

Let your team members be in charge of certain projects and outcomes. Encourage them to share ideas and give input on important decisions. Make your team's work process and strategic execution a discussion, not a dictation.

- **Get involved.** Similar to being in the weeds of your business from an awareness standpoint, be willing to roll up your sleeves and actually do the work. Lead by example. People trust leaders who are willing to hop in and run sprints with them, not just stand on the sidelines yelling at them to run faster.

- **Have work-free conversations.** Your team is a group of people not just production-based robots. Like you, they have likes, dislikes, interests, and goals. Get to know who they really are. Show an interest in their personal lives and they'll be more open to listening to you when it's time to talk business.

- **Don't steal credit.** Recognize that strategy and ideas don't actually get anything done; it's the people on your team that execute the game plan who make plays and get wins. Recognize people for their efforts. If someone on your team presents a brilliant idea, don't take it as your own—give them the props they deserve.

- **Proactively push their dreams.** After you've learned about your team members' aspirations, go out of your way to present them with opportunities to further themselves. Show that you care about their future without them having to ask you first. Take them to see an influential speaker in their respective field. Set up a meeting with them and a knowledge expert. Email them about upcoming events and workshops.

- **Realize you're not perfect.** Just because you're a leader doesn't mean your answer is the right one. And don't feel the pressure to be all-knowing. No one's perfect. Be open to others' opinions and allow someone else's idea to trump yours if it's better.

• **Put the team first.** Just like everyone, leaders aspire to continue climbing the ladder. But you're in a unique position as a leader. Don't put your ambitions ahead of the group's success, or they'll never give you their best effort. Be willing to accept all the blame and give all the credit to your team.

Focus on What Matters

You have to get to know your people. Learn from them. Gain a better understanding of their "why" for working at your company. If they just view it as a job, what are some things you can do to help them think of it as more than just a job?

At Michigan State, Coach Izzo did a great job of getting to know all 15 people on the roster, understanding what our individual goals and dreams were, and helping us try to accomplish those. The same thing happens here as I lead my Company.

I have to find out what matters to our team members. Is it the paycheck? Is it work-life balance? Discover the things that really matter to your people and then deliver them. When you deliver those things for people and help them achieve their goals, they want to help you achieve yours.

People at our Company care about their health, so we put a doctor's office in the building. They care about working out, so we set up state-of-the-art fitness center. They care about spending time with their families, so we give them a great work-life balance. They care about having memorable experiences, so we hold a Company-wide fair every year for our team members and their families to enjoy a fun night out. They care about those things, so we deliver them.

By showing our people that I care about what they care about, they reciprocate by caring about what I care about. And then, all of a sudden, they say, "Gosh, it is fun being No. 1."

A lot of businesses determine whether they have succeeded or failed based on their bottom-line financial numbers. That's not my style. The process is what matters. Does our technology enable our team members to move loans quickly through the pipeline? Is a process that is usually completed in less than 24 hours suddenly taking two days? I am in the weeds, focusing on winning, making our Company successful, and taking care of our internal and external clients. When those things happen, the money will come.

At the end of a basketball game, you can look at a scoreboard and the final score reads "71–66." But I don't care about the score. How did we play, and what led to that final score? I look at every single play and think about what we could have done differently. What went wrong on that possession right before the second media timeout in the second half? I analyze every single play and every single detail. Those are the things that ultimately result in the final score.

Focus on winning and guide your team toward success, and the money will follow. Don't ever lose sight of that extra layer of leadership that doesn't show up on the balance sheet.

Building relationships with your team members and demonstrating an interest in their lives that extends beyond their scope of responsibilities will not only make you feel better about yourself as a leader, it will also motivate your team in a way that will greatly exceed your goals.

The key to your success as a leader lies firmly in the hands of your talent. Show a genuine interest in them and take care of them. Your mission as a leader isn't to make your team members put in extra effort because you told them to, or because they feel like they have to. You're a successful leader when your team wants to have your back and puts in the extra effort because it's for their own benefit.

Fast Break Points

✓ Find out your team members' personal and professional goals and help them get to where they want to go.

✓ Provide an environment that satisfies, inspires, challenges, and gives them the resources to grow their careers.

✓ Allow your team members to steer the creativity and ideas behind your projects.

8
WIN WITH PEOPLE

AT ONE POINT DURING MY SOPHOMORE SEASON AT Michigan State, our team was going through a rough spell. We hit a shooting slump and our production in games was looking sloppy because of it.

Coach Izzo was getting on us one day at practice, challenging our commitment to getting things back on the right track.

"We're not shooting well right now," he said. "What are you doing about it? Are you focused on getting better, or are you just hanging out with your girlfriends?"

Jason Richardson, who at that time was playing around 15 minutes a game as a talented freshman role player, said, "Well, I was in here at 11:00 last night getting shots in and working on my game."

Now, you'd think that those words would be music to Coach Izzo's ears. Jason was a young, talented guy with a bright future ahead of him, so for him to dedicate his free time to putting in work in the gym is exactly what you'd think would satisfy Coach Izzo.

Not exactly.

Instead of getting patted on the back for his work ethic and commended as a positive example for the rest of the team, Coach Izzo actually showed disappointment.

He said, "That's great. Thanks for coming in to work on your shot, but why didn't you pull other people in with you? Why didn't you pull Ishbia and Adam Ballinger in with you? We're not going to get any better as a team if people are only looking to get better individually."

That moment taught me that leading by example isn't sufficient when you're trying to improve as a team. It's a cop-out. It's as if you're saying that the only thing important to you is that you're handling your own responsibilities and looking out for your own best interests, instead of looking to make the entire team better.

That's not being a leader. Grab someone on your team and tell them that you're going to the gym to work on your shot, or that you're going to study up on your company's products and services, so you can speak to customers more knowledgably the next time. Leaders encourage other people to join them so that everyone can improve together.

Whether it's a basketball team or a business, you win with people. Winning and success come from people on the same team working cohesively to chase a shared goal.

The main reason that United Wholesale Mortgage has been so successful is because of our people. Sure, we have amazing technology, but that's because we have hundreds of people in IT that work hard every day to build and enhance our different tools and platforms.

We didn't grow to become the No. 1 wholesale mortgage lender in America and set an all-time Company record for loan production by chance. We did it because of all the great work that our team members put in every day.

Our training team coaches our people to be the most knowledgeable and skilled professionals in the industry. Our sales team members build great relationships with their clients and truly focus on coaching them on processes, like a true partner, instead of treating them merely as a means to a commission check. Our underwriters review loan applications with better quality and service than any other company.

We don't have any kind of patented mortgage products that no one else has. Our people differentiate us. Nothing else.

Teamwork Trumps Talent

It is true that the team with the best players usually wins, but talented teams only win championships if there's a certain level of chemistry and cohesion amongst the players. If it's just a group of individuals playing for their own accolades, they're not going to reach the top. They could easily lose to a team of lesser talent that plays better as a unit.

The Detroit Pistons dominated the 2004 NBA Finals, despite being a group of somewhat overlooked players. They won the best-of-seven series in only five games over a Los Angeles Lakers team that featured four future Hall of Famers in its starting lineup (Shaquille O'Neal, Kobe Bryant, Gary Payton, and Karl Malone).

From a different perspective, in college basketball, the 2015 Kentucky Wildcats were loaded with talent, posting 38 wins (tying for an NCAA record), and saw four of its players selected within the top 13 picks of the NBA draft. But they didn't win the national championship. They actually didn't even make the championship game, losing in the semifinals to Wisconsin.

When it comes to filling leadership positions at companies, a lot of CEOs make the mistake of focusing solely on a candidate's résumé. They'll often conduct a national search for the most well-known person with the best track record in the industry.

There's nothing necessarily wrong with that strategy. If you want to grow your company's digital presence, it seems like it would make sense to hire the "renowned social media guru" who has transformed other large organizations and is a recognized influencer in the field.

But where you could strike out with the decision to hire the industry's big gun is if they come in and detract from the company culture you've built. A person's knowledge or influence loses its value if people can't stand being around them.

You have to get people who are culturally aligned; people who care and have a team-first attitude. I'd much rather promote people from within to leadership positions and get people that I know are team players, as opposed to going out to cherry-pick a top executive from another company.

Coach Izzo operated the same way. He knew he could go out and get a five-star superstar to join the program, but he's not going to sacrifice the team for one individual if that person doesn't align with the culture of the program. Even someone with transcendent talent would get passed over if Coach Izzo felt his "me-first" attitude would burn bridges in the locker room and hinder our ability to function as a team.

A basketball team of 15 "I's"—as opposed to people with a "we" or "us" mentality—isn't going to win a championship.

Never lose sight of the importance of team. Someone can have a great skill set and all the ambition in the world, but unless they incorporate that drive and vision into the overall team concept, your team will fall short of its goals.

Keep Your Grass the Greenest

The reason our Company is so successful is because everything is focused on delivering an exceptional client experience. That's everything I think about. Obviously, on one hand we have external clients, which are mortgage brokers throughout the country that we work with. We make sure we deliver to them the fastest, easiest processes, and give them the best technology and partnership tools to help them grow their own business.

On the other side of the client experience spectrum are our internal clients—the nearly 4,000 team members we have working at United Wholesale Mortgage. A top priority of ours is giving our people a workplace they are proud of and are excited to go to each day.

We make it a priority every year at our Company to deliver events, opportunities, amenities, and perks that make working here a unique experience, not just a job. There are cool prizes that people can win, like a day trip to an amusement park, or a cruise to the Bahamas. There are the Company fair and holiday parties, where we've had well-known performers like Nelly and Flo Rida give surprise concerts. We've had famous basketball players Magic Johnson and Isiah Thomas speak to our Company and take pictures as surprise guests at Company rallies.

From an amenities standpoint, we considered what our team members like to do on their way to and from work and incorporated those things into the building. We have a Starbucks, doctor's office, fitness center, salon, arcade, massage therapist, convenience store, and indoor basketball court—all in our headquarters. We were the first company in the country to build an in-house Escape Room that we use for training purposes.

All of those things show that we have our team members' best interests at heart and that we want to make this a place where people truly love to work. It goes beyond the numbers. If we were a typical huge corporation, I'd be more concerned about the costs associated with those things. My big worry would be explaining the ROI of an indoor basketball court to our board of directors.

Fortunately, we're a family-owned company, so I don't need to do some kind of cost-benefit analysis on the basketball court. If it makes our people happy and can be done in a practical sense, we're doing it.

The practicality is the key concern in my mind. There are a lot of companies out there that have amazing amenities. But what we focused on was delivering amenities that made sense; that made our team members' lives better.

We considered what people typically do on their way to work in the mornings, or on their way home in the evenings. We have a Starbucks because a lot of people stop and get coffee on their morning commute. We built the huge fitness center because a lot of people like to get in workouts before or after work. Sometimes, people need to go to the doctor but don't want to take time out of their work day to go sit in a waiting room, so why we put a doctor's office in our lobby. The examples go on and on.

When people are unhappy, they start looking around for other opportunities. That's not what I want. I'm interested in people wanting to stay here for 15 or 20 years, instead of just one or two. It's up to me, as the leader, to provide opportunities for fun and career development and work-life balance so that our team members don't want to leave.

Value the Person Over the Job

There are instances when hardworking, high-achieving team members actually get promoted one step beyond where they're actually best suited to be impactful. It's not anyone's fault; that's just how it goes sometimes.

As a salesperson, a role in which you are primarily responsible for hitting individual weekly or monthly numbers, you might knock it out of the park. But that doesn't necessarily mean you'd succeed in a role where you're supposed to coach other people.

That can lead to a dilemma for people, as a promotion to a leadership position is often the next career phase for successful individual performers in a variety of industries. But how do you handle the situation, as a leader, when an incredibly successful person gets promoted one step too far, and ultimately fails because of it?

A lot of places might only view that situation through the current lens and cut ties with the employee because they're not succeeding in their new leadership role. But that's a mistake. Don't kick someone talented to the curb because they're not succeeding at a position that *you* put them in.

Our Company is big on internal transfers. If someone with a great work ethic and attitude is hired into a role and, over time, it becomes apparent that they just aren't cutting it, we don't just fire them. We look for other positions or other teams within the Company where they could be a better fit and have a greater likelihood of success.

Prioritize "Real Life"

Never lose sight of the fact that, regardless of what position or title someone has at your company, their job likely isn't the most important thing in their life. Hopefully, it isn't. They are people, first and foremost, and their role of mom, dad, wife, husband, brother, or sister is the most important title they have. That's "real life" stuff.

It doesn't help that much if you, as the CEO or a high-level executive, tell your team members that their "real life" issues are priorities *to you*, but then the mid-level leaders in your company—the people they actually report to—don't act the same way.

You have to make sure that valuing your team members' personal lives is something that is etched into your company culture. Everyone has to be on the same page.

It's natural for mid-level managers to get caught up in the daily and weekly production numbers of their direct reports if they get paid to reach specific goals and benchmarks. If one of their team members stays home to take care of a sick child, there's a chance the manager views their absence more as missed production instead of someone being a loving parent. Always value your people, and their "real life" situations, over the numbers associated with a job. It benefits everyone in the long run.

In the end, recognize that your people are the reason for 100 percent of your success. Without them, you'd be nothing—no matter how smart you are. Treat them with that level of respect and appreciation, get them to buy in to you as a leader, and your company will thrive.

Fast Break Points

✓ Leading by example isn't enough. Perform at a high level and pull people along with you.

✓ Lead with integrity. Treat your team members as human beings, not just robots doing a job.

✓ Be upfront with your people and don't surprise anyone. Make your expectations clear.

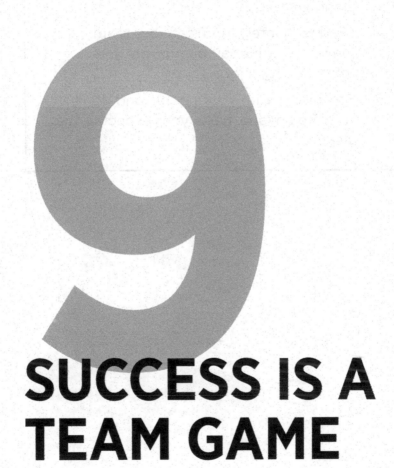

9
SUCCESS IS A TEAM GAME

THERE WAS NO QUESTION HOW MUCH COACH IZZO HATED to lose and loved to win. He did everything in his power to make sure our team, and his program, were successful, routinely putting in 80-hour work weeks.

He was the ultimate thumb-pointer. He felt that he had the ability to control the outcome of games by how he prepared us for each game. Coach Izzo would be in the film room most nights watching game film on our upcoming opponents until 2:00 AM because, in his mind, every minute he spent watching film impacted the outcome of games.

He was the epitome of a CEO-style coach, truly in charge of every facet of the Michigan State basketball program. He wasn't just an X's and O's guy. His ability to manage people, handle conflicts, and keep the team focused in its pursuit of long-term goals was remarkable.

But despite all the accolades and notoriety that Coach Izzo has earned, he'd be the first to say that his success is the byproduct of a collective group effort.

Beyond him, we had a staff of incredibly hardworking assistant coaches who put in countless hours of watching film, scouting opponents, player development, monitoring academics, and recruiting. Despite Coach Izzo being very hands-on with every element of the program, the assistant coaches carried a lot of the weight.

Over his career, Coach Izzo has earned Michigan State a reputation as a program that is consistently a top performer in the quick turnaround format of the NCAA Tournament, playing two games in three days multiple times.

Like any head coach, he poured 100 percent of his focus and preparation into the upcoming opponent. But what we didn't know as players back then was that, at the same time, he had his assistant coaches doing exactly what he never wanted us doing—looking ahead on the schedule.

One of the biggest mistakes you can make in team sports is looking past your next game. You play the games one at a time and it's important that you pour all your attention into your next opponent. If you start looking ahead a few games, or a few weeks, maybe to rivalry game or a marquee matchup against a highly ranked team, you risk losing a game that you should have won.

The philosophy was always, "We have to win *this* game because, without this win, there is no next game."

So, in the 2000 tournament, it was easy to pay close attention to our Final Four matchup against No. 8 seed Wisconsin, who we had already beaten three times that season (twice in the regular season and once in the conference tournament), as opposed to looking too far ahead to a possible championship game against either No. 5 seed Florida or No. 8 seed North Carolina.

It's really hard to beat a Big Ten team four times in a season. We knew that. We also knew that our previous three wins over the Badgers wouldn't mean anything unless we beat them in that national semifinal game.

As players, we couldn't afford to look ahead, but at the same time, given the quick turnaround of NCAA Tournament games, our coaching staff had to have a long-term strategy in place so they could best prepare the team at each step of the journey.

The tournament is set up as several two-day tournaments that take place over the course of a few weeks. Leading in to the first round of that same 2000 tournament, the entire coaching staff and all of us players were completely focused on preparing for our opening game against No. 16 Valparaiso.

On top of that, Coach Izzo gave his assistants an extra assignment to cover the other teams that we would potentially play in the second round two days later. One assistant scouted No. 8 seed Utah and another assistant scouted No. 9 seed Saint Louis. Each coach put together full, detailed scouting reports on their respective assignments, with in-depth analysis of players and team tendencies, and had film cut on each.

With Utah winning that game, the scouting report and film that had been done on Saint Louis became irrelevant. The coach that put together the scouting report on Utah initially served as our expert on them, so as soon as we got back to the hotel, we all met in a conference room and he led the meeting, discussing Utah and taking us through everything, step-by-step. He knew enough to guide that meeting; after the players left, all of the coaches went to town studying and analyzing Utah.

None of that accelerated, game-by-game preparation would have been possible without a staff of talented and hard-working assistant coaches. Just like it was important for the players on the court to jell and play as a team, the chemistry and accountability within the coaching staff was just as critical to us winning the national championship.

The business world works the same way. A CEO won't amount to much without a team of smart, strategic experts in leadership roles, and without a team of motivated people who want to work hard and bring ideas to the table so the team can succeed.

Don't Get in Talent's Way

No matter how hands-on or "in the weeds" you are as a leader, you can't be everywhere all the time. You have to be comfortable delegating responsibility and relying on other people, whether it's an assistant or other members of your leadership team.

Hire smart, talented people to do a job and then get out of their way. Give them space to be creative and implement their own system for how their team or department will operate. Let them lead in their own unique way so they can build relationships with the rest of their team and maximize everyone's performance.

At our Company, every team member is a decision-maker—and they should be. I want people to voice their opinions and ideas because that kind of collaboration and diversity of thought is what makes us grow. This isn't a company where everything flows down from the top, and we're better off because of it.

Lead at Your Level

Delegating tasks isn't just beneficial from the standpoint of giving other talented leaders some breathing room—it's also about giving yourself the space you need to zone in on your own priorities.

Despite how involved and "in the weeds" I want to be with everything that goes on at our Company, it simply makes more sense, from a workload standpoint, to hand off the main day-to-day tasks of a project to other people.

Time is valuable for everyone, but especially at the Company leadership level, where more demands are made on your time.

A simplified way of dissecting your business to best allocate time, effort, and resources at the leadership level is by broadly classifying the work your company does into different levels.

You'll obviously have exceptions, as people are paid differently, but generally speaking, there is $10-an-hour work, $20-an-hour work, $40-an-hour work, and $300-an-hour work.

It's a spectrum that ranges in intensity, maybe from administrative work to high-stakes contract negotiations. Assigning those values to tasks is a subjective process that varies from one company to the next. As the leader, you've got to place a value on the various responsibilities in your workplace, distribute them amongst your team, and focus on what's appropriate.

If you're the CEO or a high-level leader at a company, it's not the best use of your time to be doing $10-an-hour work. You have to delegate those things. Focus on what you're best at and what most benefits the company and prioritize the things that only you can do.

If there is a job that 10 people or 100 people can do, let them focus on those things. You can be in the weeds and follow up with them to ask questions, but you don't have to do the work.

For example, I understand underwriting guidelines as it pertains to the mortgage industry. I can do all that, but it doesn't mean I need to call our investors and ask for variances. We have people on our team who are very capable of doing that.

If, for whatever reason, we're not getting what we're looking for and I need to get involved, then an underwriting team leader can handle the majority of the conversations and perhaps coordinate a phone call between myself and the CEO of our investors so that I can accomplish what we want.

There was an instance where we wanted to re-negotiate our existing deal with a vendor because we had the talent and resources to build our own version of the services they were providing. That's a move that would save millions of dollars over several years.

So, we began trying to negotiate a better deal with the vendor while, at the same time, instructing our IT leaders to build the platform ourselves internally.

Our Vendor Relations team negotiated them down on price, but as negotiations drew closer to the end, I had our team pass on the word to the vendor that I wasn't happy with their service and that I wanted an opt-out clause if they didn't deliver on the service levels we were looking for.

They refused. They said that if we wanted incentives, we had to do a long-term deal and that were would be no opt-out clause. At that point, I connected with their CEO for a phone call and convinced him to give us the deal that we wanted. That's where the idea of $300-an-hour work comes into play. I got on the phone with the CEO, where I explained the "why" behind our demands.

As the CEO, I didn't need to be the one to go back and forth over contract language during the two or three months that we were negotiating with this vendor. I came in at the end to close the deal. I delegated the entire process to one of our leaders who, ultimately, did a great job, but there are certain parts of negotiations that, quite frankly, require a CEO's touch. The reality is that a vendor hearing stipulations and concerns from the leader of an organization is different than hearing it from someone else.

Hire Strategic Thinkers, Not "Yes" People

Your job as the leader is to hire great people and then coach and empower them and trust that they'll do a great job.

Don't train your leadership team to think the way you think. Train them to think how you want *them* to think. There's a big difference there.

A leadership team is most valuable when you encourage people to share their own thoughts, opinions, and viewpoints. If no one brought any original ideas to the table, and simply agreed with the CEO because they want to be seen as a team player, then there's no point of having a leadership team at all.

"Yes" people don't offer anything new. They don't innovate, and they don't move the needle. It's important to come up with ways to force people to speak up and find opportunities for continuous improvement.

One way we've incorporated that among leaders at our Company is that, in our weekly senior leadership meetings, every team is required to present to the group one teamwork opportunity that involves another team, essentially explaining what went wrong on a certain project and giving a suggestion for how the teams can work better together moving forward.

The bottom line is that you hire people, or promote people, to leadership positions because you respect their strategic thinking and decision-making abilities. You expect them to make a difference. If they just blindly follow what the CEO says because it's easy and isn't confrontational, that doesn't benefit anyone.

Challenge your people to speak up.

Just like a team won't function well unless it has a selfless "team-first" mentality among its players, the team also won't reach its highest potential unless all of its players perform to their best ability every day.

Fast Break Points

✓ Surround yourself with talented people and give them opportunities to push themselves and make their own mark.

✓ Run a team-first system. Don't make everything about you. View successes as collaborative efforts and attribute individual accolades to a group effort.

✓ Delegate authority to the people on your team. Recognize areas where others are more knowledgeable or skilled than you are and get out of their way. Focus on the things that only you can do.

10
ANYONE CAN LEAD

"LEADERSHIP" HAS BECOME A BUZZWORD IN COLLEGE *sports in recent years.* Whether it's a coach discussing the maturation process of a player after multiple years in the system, or a student-athlete describing themselves to scouts in pre-draft meetings, talking about "leadership" is growing in popularity.

But that doesn't change the fact that there are a lot of people who misinterpret its meaning. In the sports world, where labels like "best" and "most talented" are erroneously given to people simply because they're bigger, stronger, and faster, the word "leader" can also be mistakenly given out—or *not* given out—in the exact same way.

You might think that a basketball player needs to be the leading scorer on his or her team to be viewed as a leader, but that isn't true.

There isn't a right way or a wrong way to lead. Some people lead by example, while others are more vocal. Some leaders are loud and get in your face, whereas others are most impactful by picking the right moments to speak up. Leadership comes in many shapes and sizes.

I was a 5-foot-9 point guard who wasn't bigger, stronger, or faster than anybody on a Michigan State roster that was loaded with NBA talent. But despite the fact that I barely played, I was considered a leader on the team.

All of my teammates and coaches knew that I was all in, giving everything I had on a daily basis. I never relaxed or took plays off.

To be viewed as a leader, even as the 14th- or 15th-most-talented player on a 15-person team, you have to go above and beyond. Be early, do everything that is asked of you, and outwork everyone. There was never any doubt about my work ethic or my attitude. And it took years of doing things the right way before I was viewed as a leader, because you don't easily morph from a lowly walk-on to earning a scholarship and being seen as a leader on a Final Four team. You have to earn that.

There isn't a checklist of qualifications that make someone suitable to be a leader. You can't get a degree in leadership in college, and there isn't some kind of special leadership chromosome that we're born with. It doesn't magically appear because of your title.

Leadership isn't based on your weekly numbers or the number of plaques in your office. You're either a leader—or you're not a leader—all day, every day, because of how you carry yourself.

Leadership Doesn't Mean Being Loud

A lot of people underestimate their leadership capabilities because they can't see themselves taking charge of a situation and guiding the actions of others or being the person that people turn to for help making a decision.

You don't have to be an extrovert or a master motivational speaker to be a leader. Sometimes, especially when situations can become hectic and fast-paced, the best leader is the person who remains calm and keeps everyone from panicking. Simply be someone that makes the people around you better.

Anyone can distinguish themselves as a great leader in their organization by having self-respect and being self-disciplined, trustworthy, and relatable. It's an achievement you earn by the respect your co-workers have for you and how people naturally rally behind you.

People follow leaders because they want to, not because they have to. And that has nothing to do with how outgoing you are.

The Easy Path Isn't Always the Best

It's okay to think or act differently than everyone else. Don't just fall in line with what other people are doing.

Coming out of high school, I was the best player on our basketball team at Seaholm, and one of the best players in the district. But that didn't change that fact that I was only 5-foot-9 and didn't have the pure athleticism that most guys possess to play big-time Division I college basketball.

If I conformed to conventional wisdom, as some people encouraged me to do, I would have gone to a smaller Division I school or a Division II school, where I would have played a lot more and potentially been a star. But I didn't want to settle for that. I wanted to challenge myself by competing against some of the best players in the country at Michigan State, even if it meant that I only got to play in the last few minutes of games that were well out of hand.

That decision I made to be a benchwarmer at Michigan State has had a far greater impact on my life than I would have gotten as a star player at a smaller, lesser-known school.

My five years in the Michigan State basketball program were about more than a national championship ring and a collection of Final Four rings. That experience of playing and coaching for

Coach Izzo gave me a crash course in leadership that I couldn't have gotten anywhere else.

Create a System That Develops Leaders

Leadership will always be about more than production numbers or achievements, whether you're growing into a leadership role yourself or developing rising stars in your company. It's important that you come up with a list of behaviors to serve as a guide for making a positive impact on your team members.

At United Wholesale Mortgage, we have 12 "How We Do It" behaviors that our captains are expected to abide by to create the best possible environment for everyone who works here. They play an important role in sustaining the culture of opportunity, professional growth, and continuous improvement that we have built here.

As the CEO, our captains' performance in these behaviors is something I pay close attention to, beyond all the metrics and production reports, to ensure that our leaders are doing their job to develop our people. Our "How We Do It" include:

- **We Collaborate.** Work together as a team to identify the right answer and support the end result. Ask people for their opinions, engage in cross-team interaction to develop ways to improve, and explain the "why" and the "how" behind decisions.
- **We Communicate.** Open and regular communication with team members is key to success. Consistently meet with your team through daily and weekly meetings to share information and involve everyone to keep them engaged.
- **We Recognize.** Consistently recognize, acknowledge, and praise teams and individuals, both in private and in front of

their peers. Randomly spotlight someone for a job well done and celebrate small victories to build confidence.

- **We Share Success.** Function as one united team that shares and celebrates one another's success. Set high standards and goals across the board and hold teams accountable, while helping them reach their potential.

- **We Motivate.** Have motivational contests to enhance camaraderie, fun, and friendship in the workplace. Get to know team members and find ways to motivate them on an individual level.

- **We Breed Positivity.** A positive attitude is mandatory. Always support team members, leaders, and colleagues, and encourage issues to be taken to a closed-door meeting where true thoughts can be heard.

- **We Outwork Everyone.** A strong work ethic is non-negotiable. Be on time, constantly strive to perfect your craft, and encourage team members to get better each day.

- **We Coach People Up.** It's not enough to lead by example. Be a vocal leader and don't assume that team members will mirror your actions. Perform the way you'd expect others to perform.

- **We Work a Firm 40.** Having a work-life balance is key for team member happiness and company success. While you're at the office, stay focused and work hard. Winners don't watch the clock or mentally check out early.

- **We Are Experts.** Be an expert in your field, understand different peoples' duties, and be in the weeds of the business. Have a deep understanding of the industry and always look for ways to innovate and improve. Shadow people on other teams to develop a greater understanding of how the company functions as a whole.

- **We Are Friends.** View yourself and the people you work with as more than co-workers; they're part of the overall experience. Encourage participation in company events, embrace fun and friendship, go above and beyond to help others, and pay it forward with kind gestures.
- **We Burn the Boats.** Be all-in for the team. Be loyal to one another and do what is right for the company and clients. Inspire loyalty and create teams that people want to stay on and grow with.

Leadership isn't something that is created overnight. Like any skill set that is developed, it's something that takes time and practice. Other people might recognize you as a leader before you feel it yourself.

Set a goal, establish a list of attributes to guide your everyday behavior and attitude, and put effort into it every day. The leadership development process is different for everyone, but attainable by anyone.

Fast Break Points

✓ You don't need have the title of "leader" to be a leader. Carry yourself in a way that makes people want to follow you; make yourself the obvious choice.

✓ Leaders don't need to be extroverts or lead group conversations. Regardless of your temperament, maintain a high level of self-respect, self-discipline, trustworthiness, and relatability.

✓ Start with the basics: strike up conversations with people you don't know. Eat lunch with someone new every day. Step outside your comfort zone and do things that other people don't need to give you credit for.

EMBRACE THE UNDERDOG ROLE

AMERICA LOVES THE UNDERDOG. YOU SEE IT ALL THE TIME *in sports, and it's arguably most prevalent during the* NCAA Tournament, when millions of people rally behind that year's "Cinderella story."

Back in 1999, when our Michigan State team made the first of three straight Final Four trips, Gonzaga was the new kid on the block and the talk of college basketball. A No. 10 seed at the time, they put themselves on the map by advancing to the Elite Eight.

A similar story has played out several other times. Tenth-seeded Davidson, led by Stephen Curry, advanced to the Elite Eight in 2008. George Mason reached the Final Four in 2006 as an No. 11 seed, as did VCU in 2011, after needing to win a play-in game to initially qualify for the official tournament field.

Each of these teams shared a common theme as under-dogs—they were small schools that lacked notoriety but had a collective chip on their shoulders, played with intensity, and committed to doing all the little things necessary to prove they could play with the bigger schools.

There are "big boys" and underdogs in the business world, too. You have the giant, well-known brands that have become household names, and then there are the underdogs, the small or midsized companies that work hard every day to grow their business or, in some instances, are fighting for survival.

Never Forget Your Journey

Our Company started as a 12-person business that ran just like your typical "mom and pop" shop. Our workspace was an old grocery store. We had a small client base, service was relatively slow and indistinguishable, and we did everything by hand. To deliver documents to a client, someone actually had to drive there in a van and drop them off in person.

We've grown a lot since then, and quickly. Now we have thousands of team members and we're based in a 600,000-square-foot headquarters. We steadily grew our business to become the No. 1 wholesale mortgage lender in the country in 2015, and we've been on top ever since.

We may have physically and financially grown out of being an underdog in the market, but our mentality never changed. We didn't lose sight of where we came from and kept that drive to be great. Every day is a new opportunity to outwork our competitors and win new business and new clients. Our focus is constantly on finding ways to improve our business, whether it's developing new technology, enhancing our processes, or offering better marketing and partnership tools to help our clients grow their business.

That mindset is more than just a conscious decision I make every day. It's how I'm wired. It's what has propelled me for years, especially since I walked onto the Michigan State basketball team.

When you're a walk-on, you carry around a different attitude than other people on the team. Nothing is given to you; everything is earned.

I went to practice every day knowing that my physical limitations might stop me at a certain point, but that my work ethic and attitude never would. I wasn't the most athletic guy on the team, but I scrapped, hustled, took charges, and dove for loose balls every single day. I took it to the guys who were bigger than me and made them work. I won a lot of individual battles in practice against guys who were All-American players because I had that commitment of proving myself.

Working with a Chip on My Shoulder

I brought that same Michigan State Basketball level of focus and intensity to the mortgage business. From the beginning, my underdog mentality at work stemmed from the fact that my father owned the company.

As I grew with United Wholesale Mortgage, I knew it would be a natural reaction for people to view me as an inexperienced thirtysomething that was handed the reins of the Company simply because I was the owner's son.

I made a concerted effort to go above and beyond to prove that I was the real deal. Whether it was true or not, I felt like eyes were constantly on me, judging my effort, knowledge, and performance. I'm sure it can be difficult in a lot of companies throughout corporate America where people who are a little bit older and longer-tenured at their company report to someone that is younger than them.

To avoid awkwardness and to prove that my father's decision to elevate me was based on performance and a long-term vision for success, I busted my tail every day—as if I was proving to Coach Izzo that I belonged in a Michigan State basketball jersey.

I'd get to the office at 6:00 in the morning. When people went home at 5:00 in the evening, I'd stay for an extra couple hours. When other account executives made 30 sales calls in a day, I made sure I made 35.

Year after year, I was driven by the thought of proving myself to everyone else at the Company; proving that my father made the right decision.

Our Company has grown exponentially since I first started here in 2003, and as I've grown into a thought leader in the mortgage industry, I've kept that desire to prove myself. Except, now, I'm not worried about proving myself to people who work here. I'm all about proving myself as the best CEO in the mortgage industry. I'm focused on elevating United Wholesale Mortgage to be the undisputed best mortgage company in America.

I might not be as smart as CEOs of other mortgage companies. Maybe I don't have an MBA from an Ivy League school, or have 30 years of experience, but I know a lot about the business and am going to outwork every other CEO in the mortgage business. To me, it's a competition and I fight like hell to win every time.

I can't dive into the stands to save an errant pass in the office, but I find different ways to make hustle plays in the office. I still get to the office by 5:00 AM and I'll stay until 6:30 or 7:00 PM.

I film videos for social media to coach up our clients and I regularly contribute articles, both locally and in mortgage industry trade publications, to give people tips on successfully growing their business.

It's a hands-on approach that is rare among CEOs in the mortgage industry, but it's that hustling mentality that has helped me and our Company grow to be strong brand names in the business.

Score a Win Every Day

Unless you get lucky and come up with the winning lottery numbers, you're not going to achieve your ultimate goal in a day.

Success takes time. Results take a while to appear. The top-performing salesperson at your company didn't get that way because of the work that he or she put in last week, or last month, for that matter. It likely took them years to get to that point.

For a long time, no one is going to know how hard you're working or how much improvement you're making on a daily basis. You're probably going to have a few decent days, surrounded by even more bad days, with only a couple good days sprinkled in here and there, for a long time.

But then, one day, all the improvement you've made and all the things you practiced will accumulate and you'll see those good days show up a lot more consistently. Somewhere down the line, whether it's in a year or in five years, everyone will be able to clearly see the growth you've achieved.

The key to reaching that point is to look for the positives, even as you make your climb. Look for highlights, no matter how small they are. Make sure you end each day with at least one positive, one win, no matter how many things may have gone wrong. And then focus on those positives.

When I was in sales, I occasionally had the hardest time breaking through to certain clients. There was one guy in particular that I just couldn't get to answer the phone or reply to an email. But I kept pushing—not in an annoying way, but in a confident way that let him I know I wanted to do business with him and that I was going to keep trying until I did.

When I finally got an email response that said, "I want to hear more about that, give me a call at 2:00 PM," that was my big win for that day. I ended up making that call and we had a great business conversation. Not too long after that, he consistently did business with me.

Being an Underdog Can Be Good for Business

Peoples' love for underdogs isn't limited to sports. It can pay great dividends to your company's bottom line, as well. That's why so many people like to support small businesses and get behind "Shop Small" messaging.

When your company positions itself as an underdog in its respective market, consumers look at you from a perspective that is more than just dollars and cents. A lot of people are more motivated to help "the little guy" and value things like service and partnership instead of making their shopping decisions based solely on price.

If a well-known restaurant chain builds a new location next to a beloved "mom and pop" shop that has been a part of the community for 20 years, people will likely go out of their way to support the smaller business.

Our Company has that same mindset. Our business model is to do everything in our power to support the small businesses of the mortgage industry—the mortgage brokers. Everything we do is structured with them in mind. We make their jobs easier, so they are best able to help their own clients.

The big messaging that we push out to the public is that mortgage brokers are the best option for getting a mortgage. We encourage people to work with a broker instead of a big, brand-name bank or retail lender who run commercials on television.

Like with just about any industry, homebuyers will receive better client service from a small business, like a mortgage broker, than they will from the big-box chains.

Small businesses are the most nimble, adaptive to change and innovative when it comes to making waves through technology. They do more with less and are committed to giving their best effort every day because they know that their reputation and future business relies on the hard work they put in.

If you are running a small business, there are steps you can take to make progress and ultimately win as the underdog in your industry:

- **Stay loose.** It's easy to tell the difference between the large companies that give off the feel of being too corporate and bureaucratic to be relatable, compared to the smaller, more casual companies that deliver a sense of charm, customization, and fun. Smaller businesses should take advantage of the fact that their ideas don't have to go through a lengthy list of departments to get approved.
- **Be nimble.** Small businesses don't have to worry about the bureaucracy that slows down large companies with time-consuming checkpoints. They can be quick to react to industry trends and make necessary adjustments along the way.
- **Think outside the box.** Push yourself to come up with and implement the craziest ideas you can. Be bold and push the boundaries. If your industry or market typically does things a certain way, look for ways to change it up and present clients with a fresh and exciting new alternative. You could be rewarded with great prestige and business results that large companies can't match.

It's natural to prefer being the favorite as opposed to the underdog in life. It means you've done an incredibly great job and that people know about your success. People expect great things from you. Never lose sight of that inner hunger and desire to prove yourself. Keep the underdog in you well fed and you'll be amazed at how much you can accomplish.

Fast Break Points

✓ Attend events, make phone calls, and check in on things that other leaders of your stature typically overlook.

✓ No matter how big your team or company grows, treat it like a startup. Be willing to come in early and stay late. Don't be afraid of working on weekends. Treat each client like they're your only client.

✓ Say yes to every opportunity offered to you. Volunteer for more responsibility. Maintain a positive attitude and seek new ways to challenge yourself, whether it's public speaking, managing a project, or doing more client-facing work to represent your organization.

12
KEEP GRINDING

THERE'S A CONSTANT WITH PRETTY MUCH EVERY MICHIGAN State basketball game you see: Coach Izzo looking intense on the sidelines. It's practically one of life's guarantees, just like death and taxes.

Sometimes it happens at times you'd least expect.

One time we were playing against Ohio State, and Jason Richardson came up with a huge blocked shot on the defensive end of the floor, pinning what looked like an easy layup for the Buckeyes against the backboard. Then he grabbed the rebound and passed it up ahead to Mateen Cleaves for a fast break bucket.

It was a huge, momentum-shifting play. Everyone on our team was fired up, and the crowd was going crazy. Jim O'Brien, Ohio State's coach at the time, quickly called a timeout to help calm his guys down.

As Jason headed to the sidelines looking forward to getting high-fives and chest bumps from all of us, he got stopped dead in his tracks by Coach Izzo, who was also fired up, but not in a positive way.

He was upset because of *how* Jason got the blocked shot. The scouting report on the player he was guarding was that he loved to go to his left, so Jason had been coached to defend him a half-man to his left in order to keep him from going where he wanted to.

Jason didn't do that, so the guy he was guarding was able to get around him. If it wasn't for Jason's crazy athleticism, that would have been an easy two points for Ohio State. Fortunately for us, it turned into a fast break opportunity, but the main thing in Coach's mind was the fact that Jason was out of position in the first place.

It didn't matter to Coach Izzo that we were still winning the game at that point. He is always striving for perfection. His focus isn't on the result, it's on the process and the details within it. If you're out of position and are susceptible to giving up a layup in a regular-season game, what's going to happen in a similar situation later on in the NCAA Tournament?

The message was to remain focused and vigilant on every nuance. Don't get comfortable with a big lead or pat yourself on the back for too long over a small success. Keep grinding.

Don't Stand Still

If you want to grow your business or improve in your profession, relaxation is a death wish for your aspirations. The worst thing you can do as a leader is relax, because you set the tone for the rest of the company. You have to set the example for everyone else. If you hold yourself to high standards even when times are good, the rest of your team will follow suit.

Great leaders don't just hand their team an instruction manual and tell them to read it on their own. They *are* the instructional manual. Great leaders don't give their people a list of goals and say, "Go." They are at the front lines actively playing their own role in the pursuit of those goals and helping others pursue theirs. They don't take any plays off.

Make it a habit of practicing what you preach. If you demand that your team members get to work on time and leave when they are supposed to, you need to do the same thing. If you want your company culture to be about positivity and team camaraderie, you better not be locked away in a closed office all day.

You can lead people more effectively when you're in front of them. Give them something to see and follow. That's a big part of why I get to the office so early and put in 70 to 80 hours a week. I want to be that example for our team members to look to.

Granted, I don't want our people to put in the number of hours that I do because I want them to have great work-life balance, but I want them to know that I am as committed to the team as I want them to be. I want them to know I practice what I preach when it comes to work ethic and attitude.

Stay True to Who You Are

Live up to the values you want to see lived out in your workplace, not the title that is printed on your business card, and people will want to follow you.

Be who you say you are. Evaluate yourself. On a scale of 1 to 10, grade yourself on how closely you carry yourself compared to the reputation that you want and the expectations that you have of others. Once you self-identify the areas that you need to get better at as a leader—not the areas that other people think you need to improve—work hard to make those enhancements because people are always watching.

As you make those adjustments and shore up your deficiencies, you will strengthen your relationships with people as a leader and a mentor, not just as a boss figure. You've got to be willing to commit to that development and make sacrifices—not just to have the title of leader, but to really *be* a leader.

Relationships Create Leadership

Everyone is different. Some people are more receptive to coaching, and some people respond differently to being constructively criticized, especially when it's in a public forum like a basketball game.

Some basketball players, if they get scolded on the sideline of a full arena, take that challenge head on, own up to it, and improve their game, whereas others might get defensive and shut down a bit.

Coach Izzo has been the same his entire career. He has coached a lot of teams at Michigan State. That's hundreds of players that he's held to the same high standards, whether it's someone with NBA-level ability or a benchwarmer. But he treated each player differently.

Each person had different goals and expectations. Someone like Mateen Cleaves had the daily goal of being the best point guard in the country, and there were expectations of him in terms of points, assists, defensive effort, and running the offense. Someone like Aloysius Anagonye had different expectations. Coach Izzo didn't go into a game expecting him to score 12 points, but he was expected to be a defensive force in the paint, to get physical with our opponent's post players, and to snag a ton of rebounds.

Despite the fact that Coach Izzo collectively held us to an incredibly high level of expectations and made sure we each lived up to our individual standards, there was a reason he could be intense and still have all of his players, past and present, love him to death. It's because of what goes on behind the scenes when there aren't cameras around.

The Michigan State basketball program is a family. Coach Izzo would invite all of us over to his house to hang out. He introduced us to his wife and kids and we'd get to know them—and they, too, became family. He'd take us on trips to different places. It was all geared toward building camaraderie and strengthening us as a Michigan State family.

Coach Izzo wasn't just committed to grinding from an on-court performance standpoint, he was always grinding to build and strengthen his relationships with his players.

The family environment was the most important thing to him because it made everything else possible. Regardless of peoples' varying temperaments, you can speak to them a different way when they realize you care about them. When you open doors of opportunity for people, take them to places they haven't been otherwise, and introduce them to people they wouldn't have met on their own, it changes things. It creates a bond that can't be broken.

And that is perhaps the biggest takeaway that I've instilled into my own leadership style—the importance of building relationships with your people.

That's why I create an atmosphere of opportunity where people can take control of their career path. That's why we promote work-life balance. That's why we give our people unique experiences like cool holiday parties, Company fairs, and cruises to the Bahamas.

Keep grinding when it comes to making improvements as a leader, whether it pertains to how you work or how you relate to the people on your team. Be an honest self-evaluator and determine what can be done to help you reach your maximum potential, and in turn, help your people reach theirs.

Improve your company by improving yourself. Stay committed to making progress. When you grind to become a better leader, the people around you will also become better leaders, not just followers.

If you want to see change made in your business, don't look for it in other people. Initiate it yourself. If you want to have a company full of people who are grinders and put in the time to become great at what they do, be that example for them to follow.

Keep grinding. You are not your best yet, no matter what stage of your career you are in. That means that you're not yet the best leader that you can be. As you push yourself and grow, everyone around you will do the same—and that's the key to any great leader.

Fast Break Points

✓ Be an example for your people to follow. Walk the floors and interact with team members. Arrive on time or early. If you want your team to give as much effort at 5:55 PM as they do at 9:15 AM, don't leave the office at 5:40 PM.

✓ Grade yourself 1-10 on how closely you carry yourself compared to reputation that you want. Self-identify areas you need to improve in as a leader— accessibility to team members, personnel coaching, and development,

✓ Develop chemistry with your team by having fun outside the office. Go bowling, treat your team to happy hour, or coordinate a group outing to a baseball game. A close team will work harder for one another.

13

THE BALL IS IN YOUR COURT

BEING ON THE BASKETBALL COURT WAS THE ULTIMATE HIGH for me because that was when the bright lights were on. There wasn't any hiding. After countless hours of hard work in the weight room and on the practice floor, it was time to shine in front of thousands of people—in the arena and on television.

For my own experience at Michigan State, if I got into the game with a few minutes left on the clock, that was my opportunity to play to the Michigan State basketball standard of excellence. It was my responsibility to manage the offense and run the plays the way that coaches asked, play great defense, and execute the game plan.

When you're between those lines on the court, it's a completely different game. There's no hiding your blemishes. Your level of preparation, or lack thereof, is on full display for everyone to see. It's the culmination point where, after all the work you've done, the question is now, "Can you do it?"

I relished the opportunity. I always considered myself a game-time player. In high school, I wanted the ball at the end of the game. I took and hit game-winning shots, and if I missed one, I took the next one, too.

I always viewed being on the floor similar to being on stage; people came to watch me perform and it was my responsibility to give my very best effort. And when I didn't perform my best, it inspired me to go back and work even harder, so I played better the next time. If I missed a 15-foot jumper with all those cameras on me, I was going to practice that shot 1,000 times so I made it the next time I took it.

It might not seem like the last minutes of a blowout victory would demand that much attention and precise execution, but I took my role seriously.

Coach Izzo held all of us to the same standards of effort and hustle for the full 40-minute basketball game. Just because we might be winning by 27 points with a couple minutes to play didn't mean that I had the green light to lazily jog up and down the floor or let my guy get easy rebounds or baskets. But being lazy wasn't in my DNA, anyway.

I knew that Coach Izzo didn't *have* to put me in to the game, ever. I got to play in games, even if just for 30 seconds or two minutes, because I earned it. If I didn't give my best effort while I was on the floor, I might not get to play the next time. The ball was always in my court.

Business is the same way. Every day is full of opportunities for you to hustle and give your best effort. Each phone call that you make or task that you get assigned is a chance for you to show how prepared and capable you are.

A project that your leader assigns to you might seem trivial on the surface, but it's another opportunity for you to prove that you can be relied upon to deliver anything, no matter how big of small of a task it is.

Every month at United Wholesale Mortgage, we hold orientations for the classes of team members that we hire, and I speak to every one of them. I introduce myself and tell them about my background and the Company's history. I go into detail about our Company pillars and our goals, and how they can grow their career with us. I tell them about all the fun things we do and encourage them to meet new people and bring fresh ideas to the table.

At a lot of companies, the CEO wouldn't go anywhere near an orientation for new hires, let alone speak in them on a monthly basis. I don't look at this is something I have to do, it's something I *get* to do.

Employees at a lot of big companies might never actually get to see their CEO in person, but instead have to settle for watching them in videos posted on the company's intranet page.

That's all nonsense to me. I want to meet all of our people to welcome them to the family and let them know that they're always welcome to send me an email if they have a question, concern, or idea.

I have a tremendous opportunity at my fingertips, leading such a successful and rapidly growing Company that is an industry leader and always pushing to do right by our clients, our team members, and homebuyers around the country.

Our Company is full of talented, passionate, and team-oriented people that make this an awesome place to work. It's up to me to keep giving my best effort as a leader and as a person, so they are inspired to come back and give their best effort every day.

You Can Do It, Too

You can make magic happen as a leader when you're accessible, in the weeds, and play an active role in shaping the positive experiences of your fellow team members. But always keep in mind that you don't become the ultimate leader overnight.

Growing into a leader is a marathon, not a sprint. It takes time and nurturing, and often requires a strong support system to keep you going.

Plant your feet in the ground and keep pushing forward. Maintain that progress and look for little victories in everyday life. Most importantly, remember that your growth as a leader isn't all about you.

Focus on making the people around you better. Leadership is more than the authority you have over people because of where you are situated on the organizational chart; it's about the trust you gain and the positive influence you can have on other peoples' development and goal achievement.

Your main objective is to get better every day. Fight off any feelings of complacency and avoid relishing in past successes. Every day is a new opportunity and a new challenge. Maintain a clear vision of your short-term and long-term goals and stay on the path to accomplishing them.

Identify the platform that you can use to inspire yourself as a leader. Basketball did the trick for me. Every bit of success I've experienced as a leader can be traced back to those five years I spent in the Michigan State basketball program.

Now I've enjoyed some of the most exciting and fulfilling years of my life playing on two championship-winning teams— Michigan State and United Wholesale Mortgage.

This is a great opportunity I've been blessed with, and I bring a strong work ethic and positive attitude to the office every day to continue making this Company the best workplace and business that it can be.

Whether it was leading Michigan State's offense on the basketball court or leading the growth of United Wholesale Mortgage, the commitment and the grind have always been the same.

The opportunity to be a leader is one that you should be proud of and put effort into. There is more than power and a title associated with being a leader.

There is a responsibility and commitment that comes with it—both to yourself and everyone around you. You owe it to yourself and everyone you know to take it seriously and bring your "A" game on a daily basis. Leadership is more than a choice; it's a lifestyle that you adapt and commit to for a cause far greater than your own career ambitions. You can put yourself in a position to change your business and the world for the better.

Being a great leader is one of the greatest blessings you could ever receive. Whether it happens or not, or how great of a leader you become, is entirely up to you. The ball is in your court. When you get your chance to step out into the bright lights, make a play. Embrace the lessons you've learned and never relax.

Fast Break Points

✓ Treat each day as an opportunity to learn and grow. Even tedious-sounding tasks give the chance to prove yourself as a rising leader and someone who can handle every responsibility thrown at them.

✓ Go above and beyond to welcome new people to your company and to pass on the culture to them. Speak to all of your new hires. Invite everyone to email you directly with ideas or questions.

✓ Focus on making the people around you better. Have your team submit their personal and professional goals and provide opportunities to achieve them.